A
TEXAS
CHRISTMAS

A TEXAS CHRISTMAS

A Miscellany of Art · Poetry · and Fiction ✸ Edited By John Edward Weems

PRESSWORKS: DALLAS

ACKNOWLEDGEMENTS

"Christmas at the Lattimores" by Elroy Bode reprinted with permission of Texas Western Press, © 1975 *Home And Other Moments.*

"Old Mount Franklin" by Tom Lea reprinted with permission of Tom Lea.

"Long Memories" by Shelby Hearon reprinted from *Hannah's House* © 1975 Doubleday. With permission of Shelby Hearon.

"Christmas Surprise" by Stanley Marcus. The Taylor Bookstore 1982 *Bookfest* guest editorial, reprinted here with permission from Henry Taylor.

"Looking Back on Christmas" by William Owens reprinted from *This Stubborn Sail* © 1966 Scribner's Son with permission from Mr. Owens. With permission from McIntosh and Otis Inc.

"The Night Old Santa Claus Came" by Benjamin Capps, "Small Gifts and Special Memories" by Bryan Woolley, and "The Goat of Christmas Past" by Bill Porterfield first appeared in *Westward* magazine of the *Dallas Times Herald* on December 20, 1981 and reprinted here with permission of the *Dallas Times Herald.*

CONTENTS

Drawing by JOSÉ CISNEROS

EARLY TEXAS SEEMS TO HAVE BEEN HELL ON WOMEN, HORSES, AND Christmas.

A great many men no doubt suffered, too, but *that* can't be admitted to outsiders, especially if our men moaned about it.

The very first white settlers in Texas—La Salle's probing Frenchmen, who took up residence for a while on Garcitas Creek—suffered agonies for sure, and, most inappropriately, during the holiday season that is the focus of this book. Imagine a Frenchman without wine, then read this description of what was probably the first Christmas celebrated in Texas (in 1686), from *Joutel's Journal of La Salle's Last Voyage, 1684–7*, as it appeared in Henry Reed Stile's 1906 edition:

"Monsieur *de la Sale* being recover'd from his Indisposition, Preparations were again made for his Journey; but we first kept the Christmas *Holy-Days*. The Midnight Mass was sung, and on *Twelve-Day*, we cry'd *The King drinks* (*according to the custom of* France) tho' we had only Water: when that was over we began to think of setting out."

A wonder it was that those Frenchmen didn't set out on their explorations earlier, considering the depletion of their wine stocks. About a month later La Salle was assassinated, and what historian would venture to say for sure it wasn't because he served his men *water* at Christmas, even if from necessity? A deliberate campaign against wine contributed to the downfall of a head of the French state many years later.

Even after permanent settlers had come to Texas, Christmas was no bargain for a while. The nearest gift shops of any sophistication had been left behind hundreds of miles to eastward, the same as had been (so the stories say) all those lawmen who were chasing our ancestors for one crime or another. During those early years virtually all Christmas presents bestowed in Texas, even on sweet little children, were rough, hand-made items—if any presents at all were given. But those crudities must have proved satisfactory enough for the papas, who thus would have escaped getting neckties, at least of the sort worn with dress shirts. Instead, Christmas gifts were more likely to have been knitted mittens or socks—and they must have been genuinely appreciated especially during the arrival of those fast-moving northers of Texas legend, when (it has been said more than once) a collapsing temperature could freeze geese and ducks where they sat in a lake until hunters shot at them and sent geese, ducks, *and* frozen lake flying into the heavens.

Enough of those stories, however, and on to the ones in this book. The twenty-three Texas authors represented here were asked to contribute something—*anything* of their choice—to a publication on Christmas. Anne Ponder Dickson of Dallas, who had the idea for this book and who, as a native Texan, knows something about Christmas celebrations hereabouts, hoped the book would manifest distinctive "strains flowing through the stories that bind them into a true Texas book, like accounts of old fireworks displays that are fast disappearing; the sparseness of Christmases past; the heartiness of celebrations with families; the mention of some unusual but ideal gifts; [red] beans and other regional oddities on the table along with turkey and all the customary trimming; the custom of saying 'Christmas Gift;' the description of Texas land at Christmas. . . . Some of the stories ought to be personal and touching, others funny, some helpful, others historical."

It appears that the authors—with their loving, unique contributions—happen to have given her what she hoped for.

Because of my early-expressed interest in such a book, I suppose, I was asked to edit it. But as an author I know what the term "editor" can sometimes connote to our imperious, individualistic group, and with the intention of living to see many more Christmases I'd like to emphasize (especially to the other authors) that I consider myself much more of a compiler than an editor of their work. With the exception of personally correcting some obvious mistakes such as typing errors, this "editor" has allowed contributors to say anything they wanted to say in the way they wanted to say it.

You will possibly notice that Carolyn Osborn has spelled ochre "ocher," which my dictionary says (without much genuine enthusiasm) is all right. But, beyond that, she is a word artist and has the privilege, as I see it, of spelling the word almost any way she wants to. On the other hand, Tom Lea spells ocher "ochre," and he is a paintbrush artist as well as one with words; so I have chosen not to second-guess him, either.

Possibly you will also notice in here, in different contributions, references to Christmas "Eve" and Christmas "eve;" "roman" candles and "Roman" candles; "highschool" and "high school;" "alright" and "all right;" "twenty" and "20;" and so on. Don't think the editor has been exceedingly lazy—at least not any more so than you might ordinarily find him. He noticed all those things, too—and if he didn't notice *everything*, this explanation affords him a good advance alibi.

Some pieces are not really very Christmasy at all. R. G. Vliet's story appears to be six months removed from Christmas, in fact, but he sent it, saying, "It is the first chapter of a novel-in-progress (nothing else in the novel seems excerptible). Its title is 'A Garland'—*that* at least may be consonant with the idea of Christmas."

Beyond that, it sort of fits the picture of that hard, early-day Texas Christmas, when there wasn't any such thing as Christmas for many people in the first place. The story seemed most appropriate as an opening, and representative of those early, thorny days. The other contributions come closer to the Christmases that we remember, know, or anticipate. And, of course, people have differing attitudes toward, and feelings for, Christmas. All this is reflected here. I might add a personal remark: that as the father of five children (though they are mostly grown and entirely gone from home now) I, myself, do not look upon the season with the same relish I did when my parents had to buy all the presents.

The contributions, though "miscellany," have been arranged in a somewhat logical order, I believe. Both nonfiction and fiction are represented; it should be evident which is which.

Following Vliet's "A Garland" you will come to a poetic anticipation of Christmas by Gene Shuford, then encounter four entertainingly written accounts about seeking a correct gift—by A. C. Greene, Bryan Woolley, Stanley Marcus (whose association with Neiman-Marcus gives him plenty of authority on the subject), and Leon Hale.

Vassar Miller, whose crystalline work can ring with the sound of truth not everyone cares to admit, contributes two poems to keep our Christmas sensibilities where they should be. Carroll Harris Simms, Tom Lea, Elroy Bode, and Gordon Baxter follow with the bestowal of some other unique gifts far removed from today's commercialism. Then appear some Christmas memories, variously reflecting a number of moods—humorous, haunting, even sometimes hating—shared with the reader by five award-winning novelists: William A. Owens, Rolando R. Hinojosa-Smith, Shelby Hearon, Marshall Terry, and William Goyen.

In two poems Jacqueline Simon celebrates Christmas in a uniquely visible manner, then celebrates also a truth that extends beyond the holiday season. John Edward Weems presents a historical tie-in with the season, followed by additional personal recollections poignantly told by Joe B. Frantz, Elmer Kelton, and Benjamin Capps.

Recollections also figure in the last two contributions. These have been chosen to conclude the book because of their happy endings.

Happy endings? Well, why not in a Christmas book? None of the stories herein can be called stereotyped *ho-ho-ho and a Merry Christmas to you* presentations common to today's commercialism, but a number of the earlier stories have definite tinges of sadness or cynicism—representing a widespread attitude toward the season. The comparatively happy endings for Billy the goat provided by Billy the Porterfield, and for the central characters of her story by Carolyn Osborn, who survived the season (but only after experiencing great severities), should leave any reader in a pleasant mood, or at least in one that won't make the holiday season *less* endurable—if that's the way he or she looks at it.

That's all I intend to say about the contents. I have my favorite selections. You can have yours.

Some of you readers might even find a contribution or two you don't like at all. In that case, please keep quiet. Be generous, and let us hear remarks only about the writings you like. Remember: this *is* Christmas, ho-ho-ho, and a merry one be it to you.

John Edward Weems
Somewhere in Texas, 1983

to CARL HERTZOG
our good friend and esteemed
designer of many
fine books.

A Garland

I'M GOING TO RUN THE HOME MOVIE AGAIN. UNLIKE THE EGYPTIAN mummy, I ain't pressed for time.

There are three roads out of town. You drive out the one headed east. Or you can walk it if you want, it ain't all that far—Highway 43, one of those Balcones County roads through scrub brush and cleared-off sections of goat range that looks like it's headed straight to nowhere, just smack into the hithering sun if it's morning or up against the evening star at dusk. A state highway, not a Farm-to-Market road, though it looks like the Texas Highway Department has about decided it *is* one. It does have a rest area alongside, with a cement table and a green-painted trash barrel, about five miles out of town.

I think I'll walk. I love the smell of browned grass and oily, heat-pressed cedar needles. I like the prickle of sudden sweat, the thickness of the hot, still air that feels like it's holding time in a cube of packed stillness. The sky is bleached white as a shirt on a bush. Anyway, to get out of an air-conditioned car will like to kill you.

Heat lifts from the pebbled asphalt. I walk by the baked schoolground with its big stone schoolhouse the size and shape of a dirigible hanger (grade school and high school combined: I'm in its dark halls, varnished walls and scuffed, wooden floors, the noise before the bell, the green door opening onto my place in a row of scarred, initialed desks)—the same building, built up of blocks of pale limestone that look like they were quarried from somewhere along the Nile, that's been here eighty years. ALTO SPRINGS, each letter as big as a pickup truck, is painted on its tin roof, with an arrow pointing north towards God or something.

Past the gymnasium (1940), stucco fronted by a couple of junipers, the brown football field with its wooden scoreboard, a few white clapboard-or-asbestos-sided frame houses, the Mexican school. At least it *was* the Mexican school until recently: now it's piled full of old school desks and worn-out Ag equipment. Around the curve and past the trailer court on one side, its tiny stone office building set amongst brush and vacant cement slabs, and on the other side the rodeo ground, an oval of fenced-in dust with a cluster of chutes at one end. If you've seen the energy that's been in those chutes—the energy that's been in those chutes—the quivering withers, laid-back ears, the flank strap pinching the bull's dick, the kidney belt and tight britches, the spurred shoulder, fingers grabbing the surcingle—then the weathered posts and rails fencing in blank space look like the sticks and drift of the morning after death.

A few coneflowers if it's June, mesquite, cedar brush, burnt grass at the edge of the caliche shoulder, a wire fence and then a rock fence, and we turn in at the stone-arched gate.

This is where the exiles stay, the 'put away,' the ones who one way or another got so flat unsociable they couldn't talk or walk or even breathe. Some got knocked from a runaway horse or pitched through a car window, some got cramp colic and took a dose of Black Draught, some, crawling through a bobbed-wire fence with a deer rifle, settled for a bullet and some settled for one anyway, several tried to cross the Nueces or West Nueces in flood, dozens met up with a twister in 1881 (its ghost still hangs over the Plateau: every bush and tree keeps a low profile like it figured to be ripped up, and in town folks store their canned goods in storm cellars), some came down with typhoid, pneumonia, or the influenza of 1918, or membraneous croup or milk fever. . .and some, amazing grace, just quit.

The white, caliche road goes up to the top of a slight rise, where it'll make a brief circle back onto itself. The ground, littered with rocks and sparse pokings of Indian grass and curly mesquite grass, is the same caliche—a kind of clay—mixed with black, mealy, lime-stone dirt. Four acres of the cemetery are for the 'Anglos' and one for the 'Latin-Americans,' a single-strand, bobbed-wire fence in between. The Mexican side is a crowd of wooden crosses, weathered or still white, with a cement Virgin here and there. The yellow mounds, still heaped up (the spring fogs don't wet the ground more than an inch deep or the winter rains more than two inches and at six feet under the climate's bone dry, nothing rots) are covered with bleached seashells, pieces of broken glass, their colors softened by the sun, pictures of Christ in medicine bottles. The place looks like a town dump. Some plastic flowers—all the violent colors of grief—are in their coffee cans, but most, and most of the faded red and pink and yellow crepe paper flowers, scattered by the wind, are all over the place. There ain't any trees over there.

On this side it's the blue shade of cedars and the darker shade of live oaks, but even here most of the graves are out in the sun. Grasshoppers tick against the headstones. In March or April yellow-cheeked warblers build their nests of torn cedar bark in the scrub cedars, and sometimes there are doves' nests on the ground. From the highest part of the cemetery you can see the town water tower and the tin-roofed courthouse, over to the west, and here and there way off yonder on the Divide a windmill sticking up. As far as you can see in any direction the gentle, stalled swells of the Plateau lift and fall, lift and fall like an ocean sea. Days the sun goes on overhead and nights the stars, which are so close they could wellnigh scrape the top of a dead man's grave.

Like I say, lots of headstones on the Anglo side, especially those bounded by rusty iron cribs amongst the mountain laurel and black persimmon bushes at the middle of the cemetery, are dated *April 12, 1881*, the day the sky turned to boiling stone and a black arm reached down and cut a swatch a quarter-mile wide through the brush, taking half the town with it.

The earliest grave, anyway the earliest with a marker still to it, has got a headstone that, if you can parse it out of the smudge of lichen and scaling letters reads:

> RICHARD A DRIS
> CO WAS BO
> RN SEPT THE 26
> 1849 AND WAS KILL
> ED BY THE INDIANS
> JULY 19 1873

Everybody in town knows everyone here: the schoolteachers who became ranchers' wives, the sheriffs, the doctor who learned his anatomy dissecting dead Indians, the dry-goods clerk who window-peeped, the woman who grew fifty-two kinds of rose bushes and shrubs and flower plants in her yard year after year, even through the three or four bad drouths, the blacksmiths and freighters and grocers and a projector operator from the movie house, town drunk who lost his false teeth at least once a week tossing up in the early morning hours at the curb around the square, barbers, mechanics, beauty parlor operators and one who, with three on and down three, in the last inning of the ninth knocked a home run in the game with Junction City in 1923 and was "never able to wear the same size hat again." I could go on and on. The citizens here outnumber those in Alto Springs three to one.

Most of the plots on this side are family plots, squares of concrete curbing, each with a slightly lower, poured concrete threshold—like the houses Marybeth Crozier and I used to outline with pebbles and sticks in the bare dirt under a chinaberry tree in her backyard when we were four years old. The monuments are the furniture.

All day long from the four or five live oaks leaves tick onto the ground, and dark blue cedar berries drop into the grass. Slightly to the southeast of the middle of the cemetery is the Castleberry plot. It's the largest plot here—big enough for three families—but there are only five monuments on it, including the small granite block for my brother, who died at age three and a half before I was born. There ain't a tree or bush on the plot: the four tall marble shafts and the little granite block are the only things that throw any kind of shade. The lot's set off by a curb topped by a cast-iron fence just like the one in front of the house in town. The fence gets a fresh coat of black paint every eight or ten years. There's an iron gate that opens onto the plot and latches shut when you close it behind you. The name

R.G.
Vliet

CASTLE
BERRY

is set in raised concrete letters on the threshold.

The four marble shafts are exactly alike—white marble base narrowing to a four-sided column, capital cut like a dormered roof, blunt, pyramidal peak. Set in a row facing east, over the heads of my great grandpa and his two wives and my grandma, they're like the markers an ancient army might of left at the farthest point of a long, foreign country march.

CATHERINE S. CASTLEBERRY
1866–1887

ALTON TRAVIS CASTLEBERRY
1850–1914

VELMA SIMMONDS CASTLEBERRY
1862–1954

VICTORIA ANN CASTLEBERRY
1886–1907

"*Love is Love Forevermore.*" "*Gone Home.*" "*Reunited in Heaven.*" "*All Shall See God, the Pure and the Impure.*" The stone over my brother's grave looks out of place next to the four tall, marble shafts, like it was the grave of a puppy or something. Its dates are *Aug. 12, 1937* and *May 9, 1941.* The rest of the family's in town, doing whatever-all they generally do in the late morning heat. My mama's cooking dinner. My sisters are cooking for their own families or watching television. My daddy's fixing to walk home to eat, from his job at the wool and mohair warehouse.

Ringtails scream at night. Days the red ants crawl up and down their sand cones. Once in a while dustdevils explode out of an open patch of ground to spin trash across the brush and of a sudden dissolve. In winter the northers throw the sleet in long horizontal lines and in spring, for three or four days after a heavy rain, rain lilies whiten the ground. Sometimes hail scratches the headstones, but mostly sunlight scrubs them.

In a corner of the cemetery, no marker at head or foot, raked out flat and overrun with agarita and scrub cedar and mountain laurel alongside the rusty bobbed-wire fence, is another grave. It's been there seventy years or so. You can make it out: the outline still shows. The body is buried eight feet deep, a little closer to Hell than all the rest, with a cedar stake through the heart.

I don't live in Texas anymore.

5

R. G.
Vliet

Festival

Suddenly, this afternoon
the birds found the largesse
scattered by the arborvitae
across the sleet-covered patio
white as linen beneath the storm-gray sky:
vested juncos, flame-coated cardinals,
myriad flutterings of wintering sparrows
black-throated and white-crowned,
a downy clinging to the bark of the big oak,
three blue jays lost among the quail
searching the scattered leaves
beyond a drift of blackbirds
fallen from the twigged heavens—
all guests at the earth's feast
served this gray and frozen day
in the whitening world beyond our window,
our first Christmas party of the season.

Come Christmas, Come Joy

When the heart burns
in its vase of flesh
fragrance spills through the glowing room
musk, lilac, sweet pine
like the packaged incense
we broke open Christmas morning
its smoking delight
filling the whole house of our lives

oh there is more here
than even the heart knows:
the crackling sparks of laughter
the flaming twigged delight
showering fire up the open chimney
faces returned from the darkness
to encircle the tree with singing
the sobbing delight of joy
passing the burning taper
from outstretched hand to outstretched hand
setting the candles aflame
light-point after light-point
enough to fill the great black dome of the sky
with clouds of blazing stars

enough to light the small warm fire
on every hearthstone. . .

J
Gene
Shuford

Christmas Shopping: A Reminiscence

I WAS JUST SEVEN YEARS OLD, MY FIRST CHRISTMAS SHOPPING TRIP. I HAD started to school that past September and felt very grown up. I went on the shopping trip with my Grandmother Maude Cole, who was the Abilene Carnegie librarian and worked downtown and was, therefore, a citizen of that mysterious adult world which "went to work" every morning instead of making up beds and washing and ironing the way my mother did. My grandmother took me Christmas shopping on Saturday, not because she had the day off but because I did. She had to be away from her job, and she got a day's pay deducted, too. This was during the Great Depression, so giving up a day's pay was a serious and substantial matter.

I was equipped with twenty-five cents to carry in a mitten. I hated mittens, but mother insisted I wear them because (she said) I wasn't old enough for gloves. I suspect the truth was, she couldn't afford to buy me a pair of gloves as long as my childish mittens were wearable.

My grandmother and I set out early for town from the house we lived in on the south edge of our little West Texas city. We didn't have to worry about waiting for the stores to open. In those days they opened at 8 A.M. We had to walk several blocks to the Fair Park to catch the streetcar, which made a loop at that point and went back to the downtown district.

That Saturday morning was bright and chilly and, as I remember, it was the end of the second week in December. Later—years later—when I was in business for myself, I prayed for cold, sloppy weather during the Christmas season because it seemed to inspire the customers. In fact, an old, wise merchant had told me, the first year I owned the store, that I should hope for bad weather the day after Thanksgiving because that started the buying season off right.

"They *shop* when the weather's pretty—they *buy* when the weather's cold," he said. I believed him. I still have my store ledger, and on those Yuletide days when it was drizzly or mushy or cloudy, I have so noted on that day's page with a great deal of underlining and exclamation points ("Sleet!!!" "SNOW!?!") and a proud arrow drawn to the total sales at the foot of the page.

But getting back to the 1930s: my grandmother and I boarded the little four-wheel trolley on the Fair Park loop—the men who were waiting all tipping their hats and letting the women and children on first. Pretty soon we were bumping and swaying up Sayles Hill on our way to downtown. The ride seemed extremely lengthy and adventuresome to me, although it couldn't have been that drawn-out, even by a dinky trolley: the entire streetcar system of Abilene wasn't over five miles long.

We bumped our way east on South Seventh Street, turned up Chestnut Street, bumped even more bouncily over the railroad tracks, and suddenly were impatiently clanging through a crowd of Model T Fords, Reo Flying Clouds, Whippets, and pedestrians along the decorated downtown streets.

"You may push the buzzer," my grandmother informed me, and I was thrilled almost to the point of terror. Pushing the buzzer on the streetcar was definitely a grownup's job. You simply could not trust a youngster to do it. In his excitement he would always push it too soon, at the wrong corner, or keep pushing it so long that it made a continual buzzing noise which annoyed the motorman.

I had to stand in the woven-wicker seat to reach the buzzer, which was halfway up the window frame. I looked around to see if some adult was going to push it before I could, but one of the men passengers smiled at me and said, "Go ahead, son. You buzz for all of us." When the time came I hit it just right. The trolley car squealed to a hissing halt right at the corner of Pine and North First, depositing us in the middle of the street. I noticed that half a dozen others got off at the same stop and was quite proud to know that I, alone, had halted this magnificent vehicle.

"First we will go to the bank," my grandmother announced, taking my hand. This embarrassed me, to some degree—her taking my hand—although I expected it to happen. My grandmother was a most cautious woman and wouldn't think of letting a seven-year-old, even her favorite grandson, walk, detached, across the hurly-burly of downtown Abilene traffic. To her credit, she did release my hand as soon as we reached the sidewalk. I solved the problem, later, by pretending to take *her* arm and escorting *her* through the mad crush of Model T's. The traffic lights had bells on them which rang merrily everytime the signal changed, and my grandmother warned me not to ever try to start across a downtown street until the bell finished ringing.

Banks were open on Saturday, in those days—if they were open at all. The Depression had closed a good many, even in smaller towns like ours that had had only three or four banks at the most. We walked into the marble magnificence of the Farmers & Merchants Bank, with one of the officers speaking politely to my grandmother and a departing customer (male) waiting and holding the door for us to enter the lobby. My Grandmother Cole was not a woman of substance, but as town librarian, she was well known and esteemed.

Going to a teller's cage, she transacted her business, using her passbook and getting a deposit credit from the teller, who wore a green eyeshade and black sleeve protectors, and wrote with pen and ink. As we left the bank, other men bowed or tipped their hats (all the men wore hats in those days and I, too, had on a cloth cap) or spoke agreeably, which made me quite proud to have such a grandmother—and quite possibly eroded a bit of parental respect I should have had for my father, poor man, who at that particular period found himself not only without the banker's respect but without a job.

"Shall we look in at Minter's Dry Goods?" my grandmother asked me. Feeling, to make sure the quarter was still in my mitten, I agreed. We entered Minter's and I was hit by a wave of that lovely old mercantile smell which disappeared sometime after World War II—a combination of the odor of red floor sweep, crisp cotton cloth off the bolt, perfume or face powder some woman might be sampling, and an undefinable feminine odor which haunted me to the point of uneasiness—a boy intruding into this woman's world.

I chose a little white handkerchief with a red rose embroidered in one corner for Granny—which was the name I called my great-grandmother by. I handed my grandmother my quarter, she handed it to the saleslady; the saleslady wrote something on her sales slip, put everything in a small, round leather container, screwed the container onto an overhead receptacle, jerked a wooden handle— and the receptacle shot off up to the cashier on a tight singing wire. These wires ran from the cashier's cage on the balcony to every part of the store.

Every store of any magnitude at all had this overhead trolley system. In a moment, back down the wire would come the receptacle to the saleslady; she would unscrew the leather holder, shake out your purchase slip and your change, hand it all to you, along with your package, smile and say, "Thank you, come back to see us," and (especially if the clerk happened to be a man) wink at me.

We repeated the process at Grissom's, Mims', and Campbell's Dry Goods. I have forgotten, I hate to admit, what I bought for my mother and father or my other grandmother, but I do recollect asking my

Grandmother Cole if I had enough left out of my quarter to buy Uncle a present. Uncle was her only son and my favorite kinsman. She looked in her purse and said I had just enough, if I chose carefully. I got him a little lacquer box to hold small matches. Uncle, despite my pious family's concern for his health and his morals, smoked cigarettes.

At lunchtime we stood in line outside the Cave, a popular basement restaurant, and waited to get a table. People who came out of the restaurant, having finished their meal, never failed to speak or raise their hat to my grandmother. The women, especially those her age, would make some little tender gesture to me and remark on my bright eyes, or my red hair, or something other than my robustness, because I was skinny as a rail and there was absolutely no room for compliments there. Two or three of the younger women asked about my mother, "Don't tell me Marie's got the flu?" or something ominous (to my ears) like that. The truth was, as I learned years later, my mother was so humilitated that her young husband was out of work that she wouldn't be seen doing Christmas shopping with her mother. "They'd know very well where the money was coming from—my own mother, and a widow to boot," she sobbed.

In front of the Farmers & Merchants Bank and the Citizens National Bank stood Salvation Army lassies with their kettles and their handbells, ringing and ringing. I hesitantly dropped two cents in one kettle, trying to cover up the paucity of my offering, but the Salvation Army lady pretended it was a dollar bill, saying, "Oh, thank you, honey," to me. (For some reason, Santa Clauses didn't man the Christmas kettles in our town until several years later.)

The McLellan Variety Store had two fascinating machines at work: one a popcorn popper which stood on the sidewalk as you entered the north door, the other a doughnut-making machine just inside the south door. The popcorn machine had little mechanical men who appeared to do the work, turning cranks and bending over to empty the full basket when the corn had popped. The doughnut machine sent a delicious sugary fragrance all over the store and also formed an exhibit, with the ovals of dough sliding up and around from the automatic cutter, to fall into the cooking oil then be propelled, one at a time, out onto a screen to be served. We bought a sack of popcorn for a nickel but decided we couldn't afford another nickel for two doughnuts. I got to carry the popcorn sack and, of course, ate practically all the popcorn. My grandmother was very dignified, as befit a Carnegie librarian, and was careful of her actions in public. It was not seemly for a woman of her age and stature to be seen marching along munching on buttered popcorn, especially carrying the sack.

Once, as we were shopping on Cypress Street, which was slightly more elegant than Pine, the fire trucks came screaming right by us from the Central Fire Station, heading toward some conflagration and I was ready to dance from excitement, but grandmother warned me against displaying too much joy at the passage of fire trucks. "It could mean that some other little boy won't have a very nice Christmas, if his house is on fire," she pointed out. I tried to suppress my fascination but couldn't wrench my eyes away from the red engines until they disappeared. "I hope it's just a false alarm," I said, a touch too sanctimoniously to be convincing. In my seven-year-old mind I could see flames shooting out in all directions from some big two-story house. With all the occupants standing safe in the front yard, to be sure.

Then, as the December shadows began drawing 'round, we boarded the streetcar at the stop in front of the Woolworth store and headed home. The day had grown overcast and the car was stuffed with shoppers and their packages, but we were all tired and didn't do much talking. My grandmother and I were immediately offered a seat by two men when we boarded the loaded trolley. I was so weary I didn't even resent the fact that I didn't get to push the buzzer, because our stop was at the end of the line so the car came to a halt without my help.

As we descended from the trolley, the air pump going "thump-thump-tonk" under the floorboards, and the motorman yelling, "Bye, ever'body!" it started to snow. Just the lightest kind of a downy flake, but real snow for West Texas at Christmas time. A rare miracle that made the day perfect.

We walked joyously through the snow to our home, and as we were setting down our packages on the dining room table my grandmother held out a dime and said, "Here is the change from your quarter."

Dear lovely soul. Of course, there had been no change, even in those days when a quarter bought a full meal. No change? Why, she had spent hard earned and scarce dollars of her own buying my gifts, letting me think my quarter was more than covering all the purchases. I think I must have had some sense of this because I hesitated, holding the dime in my palm (no mitten). But I kept it . . . how could a seven-year-old expect to feel guilt or concern over a gift dime, even in hard times?

A wonderful experience, a distant, silvery memory to me now: my first Christmas shopping trip. And, bless her sweet shade, wherever in paradise it abides, it occurred to me only on Christmas morning as our family was opening the gift packages, who the one person was for whom I had forgotten to buy a present.

13

A·C·
Greene

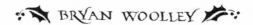

Small Gifts and Special Memories

A FEW WEEKS AGO I ASKED MY SONS, AGES TWELVE AND TEN, WHAT THEY wanted for Christmas. They thought and thought and then told me they didn't know. I was dumbstruck.

When I was a kid I began work on the first draft of my Christmas want-list sometime in August. Revision and expansion commenced upon the arrival of the first Christmas catalogue from Sears or Montgomery Ward. The cover letter, in which I listed my virtues and good deeds clearly but modestly, was composed during November and mailed to the North Pole right after Thanksgiving. Then the countdown began, building to almost unbearable suspense as I marked the days of December off the calendar and culminating in the delicious mystery of Christmas Eve Night.

It didn't matter that Santa Claus never fulfilled more than a fraction of my wishes. I was so thrilled with the dreams that *were* realized that I could forgive even the absence of the shiny red bicycle that headed my list year after year. It was the dreaming and the waiting and the mystery, I realize now, that made Christmas wonderful. And it is these wonders that are being stolen from my children—all our children—by the materialism and instant gratification that govern us now. Santa Claus is no longer a mysterious North Pole elf but a TV huckster and shopping mall shill, and he can bring the children nothing that they don't already have. He can't even make them dream or wish or imagine, and I worry that when they are older they won't remember Christmases past as being much different from other days.

I hope they will. Maybe they will. Memory is tricky. We're always forgetting things we thought we would remember forever and remembering things that reason says aren't memorable.

Despite the time and care I spent on my want-lists, I remember few of the larger gifts of my childhood except the one that never arrived, the red bicycle. Yet many of the smaller gifts remain in my mind—a certain cap pistol, a wooden truck I got during World War II when there were no metal toys, a card game called Authors. I still own a few of the books I got. But some of the gifts I remember weren't even mine.

One was a hair barrette that my brother Mike bought for my sister

Sherry when she was about six and he about eight. He had chosen the gift himself and paid for it with his own money. He proudly presented it to her on Christmas Eve Night.

Normally, Sherry's hair was one of our family's glories. It was golden and fine and naturally curly. But Sherry had ringworm that Christmas, and her head had been shaved. Except for a fringe of long curls, she was as hairless as an egg and wore a green-and-gold felt beanie to hide her baldness. When she opened Mike's gift, confusion crossed her face. Mike, suddenly realizing the gaffe, turned red. Then both burst out laughing, then we all laughed. We laughed until we cried. I don't recall any other gift that anyone got that Christmas, but it was one of the happiest I remember.

Mike was the most excitable and enthusiastic of us five children, and easily obsessed. Every Christmas, he would spend hours on his belly under the Christmas tree, poking, weighing and shaking the gifts with his name on them, trying to figure out what they were.

In those days when Mike and Sherry were still young enough to believe in Santa Claus, it was our custom to open one gift on Christmas Eve and the rest on Christmas Day, so those of us to whom Santa no longer came would still have something to celebrate.

One year Mike asked Santa for a cork bulletin board to hang on the wall of his room. While he awaited the arrival of the elf he did his usual probing under the tree. One of the gifts almost drove him crazy. It was Mike's smallest gift, a little flat rectangle wrapped in red paper. It was from our mother. One surface of the rectangle was smooth. The other was bumpy, as if covered with. . .with what? Buttons? Stones? Knobs?

The rest of us knew what was in the package, and we exchanged knowing smiles whenever we saw Mike poking and weighing it. It so baffled him that he eventually ignored his other gifts and concentrated his detective efforts on that one. He even tried to bribe some of us to reveal the secret, but we would not.

At last Christmas Eve arrived, and each of us got to choose the gift we would open early. We usually chose a gift from our mother or grandmother, a package certain to contain something we had longed for and asked for. We drew straws to see who would open first, and then wait our turns. I think we rigged the straws that year so that Mike would have to go last. And, of course, he chose to open the mysterious red rectangle. It was a card of thumbtacks to go with his not-yet-arrived bulletin board. Again we laughed until we cried.

Maybe it's only coincidence that Mike is the butt of my funniest

Christmas memories, or maybe his excitable enthusiasm for the season made him an easy victim to these small misfortunes. But the gifts I associate with him in my memory—the hair barrette he gave to bald Sherry and the thumbtacks that monopolized his curiosity—didn't cost more than a dime apiece, yet brought more joy to the whole family than a sleighload of expensive goodies would have. The laughter they inspired gathered the seven of us into the close family warmth that is always the atmosphere of the best Christmases.

It was that warmth and laughter that I missed during the most depressing Christmas I ever endured. I was eighteen, and had left home only a few months earlier to seek my fortune as a newspaper reporter in El Paso, two hundred miles away. As the youngest and newest member of the staff—and unmarried, as well—I was told to work on Christmas Eve and Christmas Day.

That assignment was my initiation into the coldness of adult life, made more awful by my aloneness. The college dormitory in which I lived was empty, except for me. Close to tears, I had watched my friends pack their cars and head home for the holidays full of joy. Even the dorm mother had left, leaving me with the key to the dorm's front door and strict orders to lock it every time I came or went. The central heating had been turned down to near-freezing. All the windows in the huge building rattled in the gloom. I imagined myself the sole survivor of some worldwide disaster, and couldn't sleep.

The newsroom was almost as soul-darkening as the dorm. Only a few of us had to work during the holidays, and the familiar clatter and clangor of teletypes and phones and typewriters had dwindled almost to nil, as if someone had twisted a knob and turned down the volume. The streets outside the window and the downtown buildings were empty. The little news to be covered—drunks killing each other with cars and guns, Christmas trees catching fire and burning children—was as dark as my mood. The guy manning the city desk brought a bottle of bourbon to work with him and drank every drop himself. I ate my Christmas dinner in a Juarez bar. You can't get much less Christmasy than that.

But sometime during the afternoon of that interminable Christmas Day, a glad-handing public relations man came up and wished us all a merry one and gave me a cigar, which I stuck in my pocket. Then about ten that night the city desk guy got mellow and said, "Hell, Woolley, nothing's going on, so why don't you go on home?"

I took him literally. I poured a Thermos of coffee, jumped into my

Plymouth and barreled off through a howling norther for the Davis Mountains and my family fireside. It was a grueling drive over narrow mountain roads through a cold, windy, black night, but somewhere along the way I lit up that cigar and belted out "O Little Town of Bethlehem." I felt as light as an angel, and it was the best cigar I ever had.

So maybe I'll give my sons something small this year, something they'll remember.

17

Bryan Woolley

Christmas Surprise

THE PARADIGM OF PRESENT GIVING IS THE ONE THAT COMBINES THE element of surprise with the selection of the gift related to the taste, interests, and needs of the recipient. If it is of a quality or rarity greater than the receiver might ever aspire to, so much the better.

This was always my first approach in solving the gift-giving problems I faced during my active days at Neiman-Marcus. There was no task I enjoyed more throughly than finding the gift for the man or woman who had everything and to come up with an idea, either so simple or so outrageous that satisfied the giver *instante*.

The late E.E. DeGolyer tried to confound me every year with his demand for a Neiman-Marcus gift costing no more than fifty cents, a limit set for the price of gifts at a holiday luncheon that he gave for a group of fellow millionaires. Even before the days of inflation, this was a difficult challenge, but we never failed him.

Other buyers wanted complex gifts with a theme that tied all of the presents into an organic unit, such as the now-famous reproduction of a Neiman-Marcus corner show window in the playroom of the late Dick Andrade, or the treasure hunt we devised for another customer with clues in the three counties, ending eventually with the final clues in the safety deposit vaults of the Republic National Bank.

I was a firm believer in the concept of multiple gifts around a theme that heightened the adrenalin flow of the recipient as she opened many packages all related to each other. I researched collections of books or porcelains or bronzes of the person receiving the gift to discover what we might be missing in a title or example they had given up hope of ever acquiring. The surprise on the receipt of such a gift was undescribable.

For a confirmed pipe smoker who had a collection of fifty pipes, I listed the countries of origin and proceeded to find pipes from four countries not represented. For another pipe smoker, I selected seven pipes in seven varying colors which were all encased in a suede-lined leather box—the ultimate gift for a confirmed pipe smoker.

Now, surprise alone is the not the most valuable ingredient. The gift must have utility and the magical quality of fulfillment of an ambition as well. One Christmas I received a pair of Mongolian geese; another time I received a jackass. Obviously, I was surprised, but I wasn't pleased because I had no earthly use for either gift. True, I could eat the geese, which I did, but they and the burro were a darned nuisance evoking aggravation instead of gratitude.

One gift I have received combined all of these elements of surprise, utility, drama and fulfillment. I had given a dinner party for a distinguished French art dealer who was making his first trip to the hinterlands of the United States. He had been a frequent visitor to New York, but he had no concept of how the rest of the Americans lived, what they ate and drank, how they entertained.

When he and his entourage of six came to our house, he was pleased to find that we didn't live in a teepee or stockade, that there were paintings and sculptures with which he was familiar, as well as works by American artists he liked but which were new to him. Our Dallas guests were simply but elegantly attired; the dining table was decorated with beautiful seasonal foliage, including bois d'arc apples which astounded him. He insisted on taking a dozen of those exotic "fruits" back to Paris with him. The menu was not the same pseudo French dishes he had been given at his previous stops, but it was corned beef, sausages, and cabbage, accompanied by a Chateau Petrus of the fabulous vintage of 1952. The food and wine literally knocked him out of his chair. "Imagine," he exclaimed, "finding a Petrus '52 in Texas in such superb condition." He was overwhelmed.

After dinner I showed him my collection of miniature books, and while he was familiar with the genre, he had no conception that so many titles in every language existed. He told me that he had a single miniature which he treasured highly, given to him by Miro, that contained an original crayon drawing and a manuscript note by the famed artist. He promised to show it to me on my next visit to Paris.

Months later, I went to Paris and was invited to luncheon at his home, which was a miniature art gallery in itself. The meal was a delight, accompanied by a variety of appropriate rare wines. When the dessert was served, it was brought in "sous glace," so that the food itself was not visible. The waiters removed the domes of the other guests to reveal an artful concoction of meringue and colored ices.

My dome was the last to be lifted, and to my amazement, there was no dessert but instead a tiny leather-bound volume neatly tied with a slender red ribbon. It was the Miro book he had told me about when he was in Dallas. Now this unique volume measuring 1 1/2" x 1" is one of the jewels of my collection.

As I approach every holiday season I recall the incident and become renewed in my inspiration to make my gifts carry the qualities of surprise, utility, drama, and fulfillment. When successful, these gifts reward the giver as well as the recipient; no place offers a better starting point to begin the Christmas search than a good bookstore.

29

Stanley Marcus

December Sunrise

It's now 5:45 on Sunday morning. I'm sitting with a big mug of coffee in a rented beach house on Galveston Island, several miles down the coast from the Sea Wall. Within the next hour and 15 minutes there's going to be a fine sunrise and that's why I'm up so early, manning the old typewriter on the Sabbath.

I can sleep any time. But I can't watch a Galveston Island sunrise any time. If this one turns out to be as high quality as others I've known, it'll be worth a few hours sleep and then some.

Four more days to Christmas. When December moves on toward the holidays and the traffic in Houston becomes a blasphemy, I tend to run. This is a good spot to run to. Yesterday on this beach I saw only four cars and three of them were parked.

At 6 o'clock there's a vague redness and orangeness in the east but night is still with me. The beach is dark except for the surf. I can plainly see the white-ruffled collars of the waves breaking on the beach. I cannot tell you the source of the light that lets me see the surf that way. Maybe its own phosphorescence.

The light in the east does not reach quite down to the horizon. Between the lower extremity of the light and the horizon there is a band of darkness. The horizon is established to me by two drilling platforms, blinking far offshore. A small helicopter made several round trips yesterday to those rigs. It was like a parent wasp, buzzing back and forth to its nest. Helicopters have always seemed like wasps to me.

I am facing the spot where the sun will appear. According to the morning paper that will happen at 12 minutes past 7.

To my right, at about 30 degrees above the Gulf, is a most beautiful great star, shining steady and clear in the blackness. I think of the square miles of Christmas lights burning now in Houston, spinning the meters of the power company. Their beauty is nothing, compared to this natural star in the east. Well, actually it's a planet but never mind that. I prefer to call it a star.

A good thing about winter on this island is that you can sit here and watch both a sunrise and a sunset and all you have to do is turn your chair maybe 90 degrees. The sun makes a short trip across the sky at this season. From my chair it seems to rise just offshore from the city of Galveston, do a lazy day's work, and go down at San Luis Pass.

Time now, 6:30. The black band above the horizon is lightening. I can see bird-shapes moving on the beach. Above the horizon in the redness there is a streaky cloud but I don't believe it'll be heavy enough to produce one of those outrageous painted sunrises. The big star is not as bright. There is time to get a fresh mug of coffee.

Now it's 6:55, less than 20 minutes before the event. Colors are changing. The dark band above the horizon—it's formed of mist, I believe—has taken on a greenish cast. The orange and red above the band have become lavender. The great star is half the size it was an hour ago. I feel a tug of regret, seeing it diminish.

I can see the beach now pretty well. Tide is out. Low tide was a little after midnight so we have a fairly wide beach out there now. The first jogger bobs past, and stirs the birds.

At this point I begin always to get a little nervous. One morning I stood on the bank of a lagoon at Cape Canaveral and waited for the space shuttle to launch and at T minus 10 I felt just this way, all full of turmoil and tension. I expect there'll be those who consider that a little too much, a guy getting jumpy about anything as ordinary as a sunrise. If so, I think they're people who never have really watched a sunrise. Not the way it's about to happen right here. There is nothing ordinary about it.

Time, 7:10. This is the point when you imagine that something has gone wrong. You've misread the sunrise time, or the figures in the paper were wrong, or else you're about to witness the greatest news story ever—the day the sun didn't rise.

Because the clouds on the horizon have disappeared, and the day has begun, and where is the sun? You're staring at the place it ought to have appeared but there's no sign of its appearance. No increased intensity of light. Nothing.

If you look away, even for a second, you may miss the first stage of the coming. If you go to the bathroom you'll miss everything because a sunrise out of the Gulf on a clear morning is incredibly fast.

First comes a tiny blob of fire. It's like a weak place that has pooched out of a bright orange balloon. And then suddenly here it all comes, rising out of the sea at an alarming rate, and it's fiery and rising too fast and you want it to wait and not go so fast and not be up and finished so quick with the rising and still it comes, and it moves toward you, and if you can sit and watch this without a pounding in your chest, well, you had better report to the clinic and get your pulse checked.

The great ball rises in two colors this morning. The lower part is orange and that's caused by the mist, the dark band that lay on the horizon at 6 o'clock. The upper part of the ball is gleaming yellow and will begin hurting your eyes even before the bottom half clears the horizon.

Every time I've seen one of these island sunrises I've tried to mark the time, and see how many seconds elapse from the appearance of the first blob to the clearing of the water. But I always get so involved in the event that I forget to count. But I think not more than a minute and a half passed during the rising, and maybe less time than that.

I submit to you that a heavenly body as big as our sun, rising out of the sea in 90 seconds, is a wonderful thing and I have never seen it happen quite like this anywhere except off Galveston Island.

You want a gift suggestion? All right, say you've got a special person to buy for, and you want a present that nobody else is giving or getting. So what you do, you come down here and locate somewhere on the beach and you give that special person a Galveston Island sunrise for a Christmas present. I did one time, and it turned out better than any gift I ever bought in a store.

23

Leon Hale

Merry Christmas From The Little Watch Shop

Give to every loved one the gift of time for Christmas,
Give to every loved one the precious gift of time,
Gold, inlaid with diamonds from the Little Watch Shop.
Remember love and Christmas, two words that somehow
    rhyme.

For Love came down at Christmas, how we're not quite
    certain,
Can't even now remember why and where it was,
But it was connected with reindeer one night flying
Till they lit atop a stable, bearing Santa Claus.

We know that love's not money, goodness me, we know it,
But some money's better, we feel it in our bones
Than no love at all, so, gift our gifts for Christmas.
In case you can't give bread, please try our pretty stones.

On Hanukkah: For Maxine And Joe

Small Jewish girl
reared in a Catholic city
you need not envy us our Christmases

outside our lighted windows
you who only observe
keep your festivals

for we are sad in our celebrations
mean with our merriments
uprooted from our families

dissecting our darkness
where Jesus sways
not on his tree but ours

here where he dangles
a little lower than his hosts
plastic and blinking

not red-robed as the Romans dressed him
still longer kept there
for all of us who now light candles.

25

*Vassar
Miller*

The Gift of Art

HERE I SIT IN MY ONE-STORY HOUSE NOT FAR FROM THE TEXAS Southern University campus in bustling Houston cursed, as I feel it, by the fact that there is never enough oxygen on my brain for me to do two things at one time.

With Christmas approaching I am trying to put on paper some thoughts about the holiday season. But every morning since November I have been getting up in the middle of the night and catching the 4:35 a.m. Southmore bus to get to a stop at West 34th and Hempstead Highway. There I get off and walk a quarter of a mile along 35th to an art foundry where I am working on a modest sculpture commission. When I return home and try to collect my Christmas thoughts I realize that, at present anyway, I seem to be able to tote only one sack of potatoes at a time. My mind wants to stay on the sculpture.

My regular job is teaching art to students, virtually all of them black (as am I), at Texas Southern University. That is within walking distance from my home. I credit my thus-far longevity to the fact that I take public transportation whenever I have to travel far in Houston. I am not an automobile driver.

Nor am I a writer. But someone has asked me to write about Christmas. Christmas as I remember it. That almost forces me to leave this busy, overbearing metropolis, at least in my brain which currently seems strapped for oxygen, and to go back to Bald Knob, Arkansas, where I was born April 29, 1924.

That was a cotton-belt community sixty or seventy miles northeast of Little Rock and near the Ozark foothills. My maternal grandparents, Major and Estella Nadine Harris (she was the daughter of a Choctaw Indian) raised my sister Montene and me. Daddy (as I called my grandfather) was illiterate, and I suppose that because of this he was especially aware of the advantage of an education. He and my grandmother were sincere Baptists, and they always made us feel that some day a way would be provided for us to leave home (an economic necessity mutually), that some day God through His goodness would make available to us an education.

Meanwhile, the kind of love they gave us took off some heavy loads. Living with them was a warm, affectionate experience. It was an environment I miss today.

Life was hard, I see now, but I didn't know any better. My grandparents always told us we should be proud of being Negroes—and *that* was the word used, not *blacks*. They told us we should never be ashamed of having picked cotton and strawberries, of washing and ironing clothes, of emptying the pee-bucket and the slop-jar, and of toting wood, and of praying and calling on the Lord when in trouble.

We were taught that the South was our homeland and that when we got the education which God would somehow deliver to us, we should stay in the South afterward and strive to better the condition of other Negroes by teaching them.

I am not one to believe that unjustness in the past should be dwelt upon or avenged if there is a good attempt to rectify it, but I will say that white men and white cotton ruled that region—by the way, Bald Knob was a part of *White* County, Arkansas—and the demands of both on black residents, and even some poor whites too, were excessive, as I realize now. We had a garden, a few farm animals, and a knowledge of homemaking; otherwise, we and a lot of others there probably wouldn't have survived.

27

Carroll
Harris
Simms

The homemaking probably led to my first interest in art. In those cold winters quilts were an absolute necessity, not a luxury. But the old women used imagination to make them into minor works of art. They also embroidered pillow cases and tea towels. One day I said to my grandma, "Show me how to do that." And she did.

Well, those days, and my grandparents, are gone now, except in memory, and I won't dwell on them any more except to say this. In September of 1938 our natural mother came back to Bald Knob and took Montene and me to Toledo, Ohio, to live with a great-uncle. There the prophesy came true. We got a chance at education. At Scott High School in Toledo a white teacher, Miss Ethel Elliott, saw in me some sign of talent, and she helped me into the formal study of art. Eventually I attended Hampton Institute on a scholarship.

Anybody who is interested at all in the details of this can read the text of *Black Art in Houston: The Texas Southern University Experience*, by John Biggers and Carroll Simms, with my friend Ed Weems as helper with writing the text. That book was published by the Texas A&M University Press in 1978. A few minutes ago I turned to it and thumbed through some pages, to get ideas about what to say in this Christmas piece, and you can see here what has developed from that.

Some of this information appears there, too, but in greater detail and somewhat different wording.

Just as I'd hoped, my memory, having been thus stimulated, has opened a flow from Christmases past, and I've recalled events not even recorded in the book—events that go all the way back again to Bald Knob. I said I was finished dwelling on them, but I also said I'm no writer; so I have an excuse for bringing them up again and destroying any continuity that you might have noticed so far.

A recollection that just now came to me:

Sometime around the second week in November, back in Bald Knob, we began gathering pecans and other nuts of all sorts, and storing them in tow stacks placed under the cooking table in the kitchen. They would be used in the Christmas stuffing and in other dishes. When the big day arrived it brought forth the necessity of killing a goose, which we had instead of a turkey. My sister and I helped to pick the feathers, which were saved to go into a pillow. Grandma used the goose fat to make a salve.

A few days earlier than that some of us would have driven a wagon into the Ozark foothills and gathered bunches of cedar, pine, and holly to make house decorations. Strings of popcorn wrapped around the tree represented snow.

Our annual school play came on Christmas night. In mid-October we would have been given lines to learn, and we would rehearse them often in our one-room schoolhouse. Finally, after a big Christmas dinner and after opening whatever home-made presents we might have received, we people of our community would gather in *our* church, Pleasant Grove Baptist (the Methodist Church being too small) and we students would reenact the sacred story of Jesus' birth.

My task was two-fold: to learn my lines and to design angel wings, a manger, shepherds' staffs, and other such things, from cardboard boxes, colored construction paper, and flour paste.

The art work was more fun for me than the dramatic performance. I was always the victim of stage-fright, and I had to struggle to avoid forgetting my lines.

In my adult years Christmas became more sophisticated. I have studied at Cranbrook and in West Africa and have completed sculptures in Great Britain and elsewhere as well as in Houston.

I have enjoyed British Christmases twice. The first time I was largely on my own and spent part of the holidays rollicking in pubs and listening five times to Handel's *Messiah* performed by a superb choir and the London Symphony.

The second Christmas I was entertained in the Edinburgh, Scotland, home of the Reverend Elliott James Mason and his wife, Geraldine, who encouraged me (about 1954) to apply for a Fulbright Scholarship that resulted in my studying at Slade School of Art, University College, London, under British sculptors F.E. McWilliam and Reginald Butler, and Slade principal, Sir Henry Coldstream.

That Christmas surely was one of the most significant ones in my life, combining as it did celebration of the season with my career in art. Later I did return to the South, as my grandparents had urged, and I have tried to improve the condition of young blacks by teaching them.

I find that because of a historical paucity of education they have a language problem—as I do still. (I'll have had help from Ed again getting this piece in order. These are, however, *my* thoughts, typed as I sit here in my one-story house near the Texas Southern University campus.) But art can outweigh language problems.

I've heard that Brueghel was said to have been illiterate. Still, anyone can look at his paintings and enjoy them. People with language problems but with appreciation for good music can enjoy Beethoven.

Looking at the works of my art students, no one could tell they didn't have at least average use of the language.

I have a conclusion to all this before I retire and sleep for a while until I rise and catch the 4:35 a.m. bus again tomorrow for West 34th and Hempstead Highway.

It's through art that people can identify. If in the real world we can never bring order, we *can* bring it here. I consider the greatest Christmas gift I ever received to have been education and particularly the training in art that followed the days of my boyhood among those old quilt-makers and embroiderers of Bald Knob, Arkansas, and I hope I have shared the gift to God's satisfaction.

29

Carroll
Harris
Simms

Drawing by TOM LEA

Old Mount Franklin

I first wrote this in order to speak it on a radio broadcast in December of 1951. Two years later I revised it a little, to accommodate speaking to the requirements of television cameras which had joined the microphones at KTSM. Since then the words here written seem to have become an invariable part of an annual ceremony, an affectionate salute repeated each year, spoken in a December dusk when a star is lighted on a mountainside and Christmastime comes again at the Pass of the North.

OLD MOUNT FRANKLIN IS NOT A PART OF ANY FABLED RANGE OF Delectable Mountains graced with green trees and softened by the fertile rain.

Mount Franklin is a gaunt hardrock mountain, standing against the sky like a piece of the world's uncovered carcass.

Mount Franklin is a ridge of rock rising like a ragged wall along the flank of a desert river.

The shape of Mount Franklin is a jumbled set of wedged pyramids, broken and interlocked, buttressed and bastioned together in a massive long line of heights and hogbacks.

Mount Franklin is built of humped twists and folds of mother rock, laced and interleaved with a little thin soil, pushed up in some primal birthpain of the earth, and then tilted above the desert's floor.

The plants that grow along Mount Franklin's slopes are tough plants, with thirsty roots and meager leaves and sharp thorns that neither hide nor cover the mountain's rough rock face. Mount Franklin is a lasting piece of our planet, unadorned.

The bulk and substance of it stand changeless, immortal to our mortal eyes. Yet the color of Mount Franklin is as various, as transient, as its shape is eternal. Let your eye follow the speckled sandy fold and slope of the hills to the level lines of the mesa tops, up the ridges, along the mountainsides, to where the bare rock stands faintly stained with red of iron, touched with subtle ochre, ribbed with rich blue of shadow, paled with high blue of distance. In the air of the desert, sun and shadow and cloud and haze change the monotone of tawny tan ground and grey rock into bluing hues of an infinite subtlety, as if soil and stone might borrow the magic airiness of the sky.

Under the journey of the sun whose shifting slants of light are never still, whose slowly shortening and lengthening shadows are always various, the passage of each moment of time casts its own color upon the mountain's face. The hours write upon it with light

32

Tom
Lea

and space in an evanescent hand, from the first reaching sunrays pink on the summit stones lifting from deeps of shadow, to the flat and formless glare of moon glittering on the grain of granite and hot in the dust, to the last glow of cloudlight touching down at day's end upon darkening slopes. Above the black loom of Mount Franklin at night, the stars wheel the never pausing mark of time.

The seasons touch at the mountain's rigid face. Spring winds make a brown ghost of Mount Franklin under the gritty amber of the sand-filled sky. Summer rain brings a burgeoning green velvet fuzz along the rounded tilt of the sun-worn slopes. Autumn haze shrouds Mount Franklin's feet and touches canyons with a blue and violet mystery. Winter snow traces with a delicate white the lift and turn of the ridges.

Above the Rio Grande's ribbon of green, forming one side of the portal of the Pass of the North, Mount Franklin is a presence and a personality. Standing above us, above the build of our town, Mount Franklin is the landmark and the trademark of where we live.

And it is more.

"A mountain," Carl Sandburg said, "is something that's fastened down, something you can count on." By that token, a mountain is a talisman in our hearts. In looking at Mount Franklin, up there, we lift our eyes toward the sky.

33

Tom.
Lea

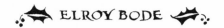
Christmas With the Lattimores

IT WAS FIVE O'CLOCK ON THE AFTERNOON OF CHRISTMAS EVE AND I WAS taking a walk through the quiet neighborhood of the Lattimores. I had left them in their front room, reading, each under an identical floor lamp with a red shade, each just an arm length away from a bowl of Dutch apple cookies set between them on the coffee table. Karen was reading *Tristram Shandy* and Philip was, as he called it, "doing his Christmas Dickens." This year it was *Bleak House*.

I had come to like the Lattimores and their sane, comfortable routines. With their books, their music, their aristocratic aloofness they managed to insulate themselves rather nicely from the ragged edges and blind alleys of the world. Life seemed to be a wholly manageable affair within the walls of their duplex—as if they had prudently taken out insurance against Mayhem and General Disaster.

So I had decided not to go home for Christmas. Instead of driving the 500 miles back to Kerrville I was glad to stay there in El Paso and visit the Lattimores, in a household that was not Christmas-frantic, that did not even have a tree or holiday decorations. I was glad to take Christmas casually for a change—with just the three of us around the table with glasses of wine and a baked turkey and normal, un-Christmas talk. Perhaps after supper we would take a leisurely drive in the Lattimore's Volkswagen to look at things around town: the big star on the mountainside, the nativity scenes in the plaza, the *luminarias* bordering the roofs and yards of houses. And Christmas Day would follow the same slow-paced but convivial pattern: we would talk books and eat well and play with the Lattimore's sleek little dachshund on the living room rug.

Yet as I walked the darkening streets of Loretto Place I knew that, for the moment at least, I was glad to be away from the too-secure atmosphere of the Lattimores and was out where the rest of the world lay in all its disordered richness. Feeling almost guilty—like someone who had sneaked off from the serenity of heaven to breathe once again the heady air of earth—I strolled past the familiar sights of Christmas eve: houses filled with squares of light; children racing across yards, showering the faded grass with their quivering sparklers; cardboard reindeer with slender black hoofs mounting the sides of cardboard chimneys. Music flowed over the streets—drifted and swelled and faded in an endless tranquil wash of carols. Women clattered down sidewalks in brisk heels; dogs barked; doors slammed. Exploding firecrackers kept up a steady, loose-jointed rhythm.

If it had been an ordinary Christmas I would have been caught up in the heightened mood of the town and the season. I would have pushed my hands deep into my pockets and breathed fully of the chilled air and probably felt a row of goosebumps climb my spine and explode a little across the back of my neck. I would have sighed or smiled, finally giving in to the Christmas emotions that stirred up visions of home.

But as I listened to the carols and watched families gathering in close for the night, I felt that everything was remote, dimly veiled. Christmas eve was charming, of course, as always, but somehow it was—*irrelevant*, if that was the word. I didn't know. . .perhaps I had simply grown disenchanted with rituals, with family reunions, with the past. I kept walking, trying to think about it: I gazed at the uncluttered geometry of El Paso streets and sky and smelled the clean air that was now full of such an even, subdued light; I looked at the mountain ridges to the north and east that made their elegant pink boundary. . . . .Yes, there was no doubt: I was glad I was not going home this Christmas. Let me take Christmas on my own terms now, I thought. Let me switch mistletoe and fruitcake for clever dachsunds and *Bleak House.* For whatever it is worth, let me just *be*, in the present, with no thoughts of the future and no memories of the past.

North of Loretto Place the streets sloped upward to a narrow prominence where the very well-to-do lived among large trees and imposing homes. Here the lawns and garden walls and flat roofs of rambling stucco houses were bordered at Christmas with neat rows of many small paper bags filled partially with sand—the *luminarias* of the Spanish southwest. Inside the sacks were single squat candles that were lit after darkness came and left to glow wanly yellow through the night.

As I walked along the top of the hill dusk was still a dim aqueous blur of trees and yards and houses, and at first I did not see the dark-robed young man standing alone inside the iron fence of the Franciscan seminary. In fact, I had forgotten the seminary was there at all: a great two-story, red-tiled building secluded among elms and salt cedars and rambling desert gardens. The priest was standing on one of the walkways that circled through the grounds, his hands clasped behind his back, his head inclined slightly downward. I could not tell if he was meditating or just standing very still—attentive to the moment when day passed into night. Curious, I stopped and watched him. . . .He seemed immensely private—isolated within his high iron fence from the rest of Christmas eve. Was he content? What exactly did such a solitary young man think about on a night like this—Bethlehem and the Son of God? When the *luminarias* were lit in a few moments and cars with their lights out began to cruise past the glowing yards, would the young father continue to stand there, gazing ahead, or would he walk back slowly to the dark seminary building and—against his will—yield to some overwhelming personal remembrance of family and home?

Paused there on the hill, I kept staring at the lone Franciscan father beyond the gate, wondering about him. Then, as if a huge blood vessel had suddenly dilated in my chest, I felt pouring through me the faces and scenes of my own past—the boyhood Christmas eves when it had finally reached the point of first darkness and our porch light had been turned on to welcome relatives as they began to arrive. I saw them all: the rancher uncles, Grandpa—coming slowly down the walk, their boots shining in brief streaks out of the dimness of the yard; Gram, compact and erect, bundled neatly against the December night air and watching for loose boards as she stepped carefully from the walk onto the porch. Soon everyone was there—all the aunts and uncles and cousins—except Mitch, my bachelor uncle from the oil fields of South Texas. It was his tradition to be late, and when he finally did arrive he would always be loaded down with presents and bottles of whiskey and sacks of fireworks: a big genial man in a huge Stetson and bulky corduroy coat who seemed to be the actual spirit of our family gatherings when he walked through the gate. Later on in the evening he would lumber out into the front yard smoking his long sweet-smelling cigar and pull out of his paper sacks all manner of whirling, screaming, exploding gadgets, and he would stand there underneath the shadowy oaks laughing and coughing and getting choked on his own cigar smoke as the Roman candles swooshed above the vacant lot across the street and the baby giants opened thunderous little holes in the sky and all of us children in the yard ran around holding our ears, grinning and pretending to be scared. . . .

I could see the food spread on the living room table and the big cedar tree standing in the corner—reaching almost to the ceiling, ornamented with icicles smoothed out from the year before and a big lopsided star and loops of old-fashioned, red-and-green rope decorations. And I could see again that special moment after supper when everyone gathered in the living room with the lights turned out: when things got quiet and finally there was a knocking at a side window and a deep loud voice saying "Merrr-rrry Christ-maaas." The women looked over to where all of us small, awed, wide-eyed children were sitting on someone's lap and, leaning toward us, said in loud whispers: "Why, guess who *that* is. . .that must be *Santa Claus*!" And the cousin or uncle who had slipped away earlier to tie on pillows and a mask would say a few more deep-voiced words through the window about presents and good little boys and girls, and then the lights were turned on and gifts were handed out from beneath the tree. Piles of wrapping paper grew between the chairs; the house was filled with laughter and exclamations and thank-you's. And always before the exchanging was done, someone—usually an alert niece or nephew— had to say loudly above the noise: "Oh, no, Uncle Esley, those are for Suzanne. . .the *baby*; there are *your* presents over *here*." And the old man, nearly blind, would take the toys from his lap and put them down carefully beside his chair.

When I came down from the hill it was fully dark. I had been gone an hour or more—longer than I had intended—and I walked fast toward Loretto Place. I could visualize the Lattimores still sitting in the living room beside their lamps. Probably nothing had changed since I left except that the bowl of Dutch apple cookies would be empty. Karen would have checked twice on the turkey and both times would have found it baking along right on schedule (rising with her book in her hand, she would have opened the oven door in the kitchen, briefly tested the turkey, and returned to the living room without once losing her place in *Tristram Shandy*). Philip had probably gone into the study several times to check his Oxford Dictionary for a couple of names—perhaps "Cursitor Street" and "Chesney Wold."

After I reached the Lattimores' house I crossed the lawn and stood beside the front yard hedge where I could see the Lattimores through the window. Both were still reading. I lit a cigarette and remained there by the hedge, looking out to the dark street. Fragments of Christmas carols were coming from the house next door and a few church bells rang in the center of town. Two blocks away on a thoroughfare, trucks lunged away from stop lights and brakes squalled in the steady Christmas traffic.

Standing there, smoking and listening to the carols, I had a curious little vision of freedom: I was a lone black-robed puppet with strings trailing at my feet. My hands were clasped serenely behind my back, and I was striding down the wide streets of heaven. All around me trees were bursting with voluptuous, storm-green leaves; whipping-cream clouds were piled on top of one another far into space; the sun was a blazing Van Gogh flower spreading golden light. Everywhere I looked the world was glorious, yet each time I tried to reach out and touch a part of it—a rock, a face, a piece of wood—my hands would not move. Their strings did not lead anywhere; they could not be manipulated.

I let my cigarette drop to the grass and I rubbed it out slowly with my heel. I started toward the porch but changed my mind and crossed over to the living room wall where a long vine was growing. I pulled off a piece of it and twisted it around into the general shape of a wreath. I looked at it in the dark a moment, then went to the porch and rang the bell. The dachshund barked from inside, and after a moment Philip Lattimore stood in the open doorway. I smiled and held the circle of vines toward the living room light. "For your house," I said.

38

Elroy
Bode

Rogers' Gift

ROGERS' CHRISTMASES WERE BLEAK. HE CAME FROM A BLEAK PART OF Texas during a bleak time of the great depression. Only we didn't call it the depression while we were in it, we called it "hard times."

The very earth was hard near Hillsboro where Rogers was born and grew up. There was rock scrabble and limestone outcroppings. Only fifty miles eastward the lush rain forests of the great piney woods began, but here at Mexia and Hillsboro the oaks were stunted and wind toughened and grew in the mesquite brush and the little boys grew up the same way. Here was where West Texas began. It was tough, and the people were somehow proud of it.

They were waste-not want-not people. Their farms and cabins and towns were weathered and severe but you never saw trash blowing along the way. Not then, not now. Their overalls were faded and old, but they were clean and the patches were of fine stitching.

The tin roofed cabins were bake ovens in the summer, and winter lay cold and bare upon the floor as it did upon the land. But Rogers had his values. He could go out in the silence of winter and still-hunt. That means that the boy and his treasured rifle were quieter than a deer. He wasted not shot nor game. The meat was for the table.

In his later years, in his fine home near the University on the good side of Dallas, he would tell of this to the young men, and they would listen in silence and respect.

I could see young Rogers in my mind, the hard Y of his shoulders and slim waist, his narrowed blue eyes and squared jaw. He had that Central Texas way of thinning his lips and turning the corners of his mouth down when he smiled. Nothing was given away. He still moved across the fine carpet of his home silently, his weight in line, as if he were still-hunting and the snap of a twig would be a great loss.

In these latter day times when all the family would gather at Christmas, he had a way, without a word nor a gesture, of showing his great contempt for the whole Christmas folly. Christmas was for children, and he never was a child.

None of this was wasted on his wife Sally, still trim, still a saucey blonde as they moved into their sixties. Rogers would fill his corner of the house with cold contempt for Christmas, she would fill all of the house with the smell of her delight in traditional Christmas cooking and having her family all about her. It was, for any who took this seriously, a Christmas Cold War.

Right at the peak of the gift giving, with everyone about the Christmas tree which was decorated by the fine hand-made ornaments that she so much loved to do, Rogers would harrumph, clear his throat for silence, and tell how when he was a little boy that all he got to play with one Christmas was a door knob and a clothes pin. The story was so utterly sad, and told with such utter faithfulness just as someone had unwrapped a bright and expensive gift, that it began to draw laughter. The door knob and clothes pin of poor little Rogers became a Christmas tradition.

Some one of us should have given him one, expensively wrapped, but Rogers became suddenly and terribly ill and spent his final Christmas in the hospital knowing full well that his days were coming to a close.

Even here the flint in the man surfaced. When a man has set his heart to the terrible business of dying well there are no words to be said, not even among the closest of his own.

He asked Sally for a party. A party seemed like the most unexpected thing this reserved man would want. This man who scoffed at Christmas, who claimed that turkey was just another bird and sea-gulls and sparrows are birds too, and all he wanted was a pot of red beans. Without fail, a special side dish among all the great cooking and baking of Sally and her daughters, there would be a pot of red beans. Rogers ate them.

And this fine woman, now heavy in her grief, gave her husband the party he asked for. He had come home from the hospital. He had come to die at home in his own bed. The party was a list of all his old oil field cronies.

They came from near and far. A thin, wraith of a Rogers got up, embraced each of them briefly. One wrote back, "Only you would have the guts to stage your own wake while you could still sit up and enjoy it. . ."

And in the business of closing out their affairs, his oldest daughter asked her dying father for his secret recipe for his hot sauce. Hot sauce and fierce cups of black coffee were Rogers' only adventures in the woman's world of the kitchen. He wrote the recipe down in his fine hand and gave it to her.

Last Christmas Rogers was gone. Gone from his favorite chair by the decorated tree. Gone from his role of handing out the gifts, one by one. His swarming and beautiful grandchildren did that last Christmas.

I missed his surly ways there. He used to not open his gifts as the others did. He just let them pile up beside his chair, carefully ignored. His oldest daughter, my wife, explained that he pretended not to enjoy getting gifts, but that he was generous and enjoyed giving them. She could never understand why. I told her that this was the way of the little rock hard boy-men of Hillsboro. That it was all a part of the no longer useful parent scripting of "cowboys never cry." I may or may not have been right. Who knows another man's mind?

We carried Rogers back to Milford and buried him there. Buried him in pure white limestone. They had to blast his grave out of the earth with dynamite. We all agreed he would have liked that. Nothing was supposed to be too easy.

And last Christmas, missing him terribly, my wife unfolded his hand written note on the hot sauce recipe. As she began to make up a batch, the recipe makes about a gallon of the stuff and a tip of the teaspoon taste will hold you for awhile, she began to suspect that he did not give her all of the makings, or had deliberately put it together wrong. Sort of one of his last practical jokes from beyond. She called the other womenfolk, but nobody else had Rogers' secret recipe. No help. So my Diane went on with the mystic work in the kitchen. A kitchen at Christmas, filled with her and her father. Her plan was to bottle it into little jars and give Rogers' Secret Hot Sauce as gifts.

It turned out to be delicious. No way you can describe a thing like this, but I asked her if we could publish his secret recipe. A gift to all of you from Rogers this Christmas. Better than a door knob and a clothes pin, but not much.

ROGERS' SECRET HOT SAUCE

4 large fresh jalapenas
1 large stalk of celery
5 lbs carrots
4 large onions
2 fresh garlic pods
1/2 heaped cup of sugar
1 pint of distilled vinegar
(not apple cider vinegar)
2 quarts of tomato sauce

Fine chop all the ingredients, grate the carrots, add salt and pepper to taste. Boil 30 to 40 minutes.

A relish to be served on meat, eggs, beans, chips, or a bar-b-cue booster.

A little bit of "hot stuff" from the lean hard land where West Texas begins.

Looking Back On Christmas

CHRISTMAS THAT YEAR, NOT ONE TO LOOK FORWARD TO, WAS ONE WE could always look back on.

On the day before Christmas Eve, my mother said at breakfast:

"How'd you like to go to your Aunt Niece's for Christmas?"

We had not seen them since fall, and it was our time to visit them. She had not asked us for Christmas, but, in the way of Pin Hook, we knew she would have if she had thought of it, or had taken time to write. There was no way to let her know we were coming. Anyway, it would be fun to surprise her driving up in the wagon.

Christmas Eve morning we were up before daylight, shouting "Christmas Eve Gift" to each other, laughing, hurrying to get the wagon loaded and on the road. It was ten miles to Novice. The trip over muddy roads could take all day or more, and there might be no passing at all on the lane from the main road to Aunt Niece's house.

We hurried, but the sun was high before we were in the wagon, with my mother driving, my grandmother on the springseat beside her, and the rest of us in the back among the quilts and pillows, the jars of canned plums and peaches, the boxes with pies and cakes.

The road was rough, the horses slow enough for us to hop out and stretch ourselves with walking. The sun was already to the west when we passed the Walnut Ridge schoolhouse. It was no more than a hand high when we came to the lane where we would turn off. The mouth of the lane was at the top of a long hill that began at Nolan Creek. Another wagon was coming up the hill, close enough for us to see a man and woman on the springseat, and children behind them on kitchen chairs.

There were two houses close together on the lane, both made of boxing planks, both unpainted but weathered a soft gray. We passed the first, the old Kitchens home place, where Aunt Sis, Uncle Charlie's sister, a strange, silent woman, lived alone, shut up in the house most of the day, summer and winter. Uncle Charlie and Aunt Niece lived in the next—a house with one big room, a shed room for the kitchen, and an open front porch.

We stopped at the front gate and Monroe got out to open it. It was a wide, heavy gate made of oak timbers fourteen feet long and an inch thick. We had passed through the gate and closed it behind us when the front door opened and Aunt Niece came out to the yard gate to meet us.

"Christmas Eve Gift," she called, her soft voice raised as much as she ever raised it.

My grandmother first out of the wagon ran toward her.

"Well, give it here."

They were laughing and crying, hugging and kissing. By the time we were out of the wagon, Austin and Ruthie came around the house.

"I told you somebody was coming," Aunt Niece said to them. "That old rooster's been crowing all morning."

While they were getting hugged and kissed, the other wagon stopped at the gate. Aunt Niece saw them and started toward them.

"It's Sallie and her folks, come to spend Christmas."

Sallie Holmes was Uncle Charlie's sister, and she was there at the front gate with her husband and seven children. I saw the look on my mother's face and knew we might turn right around and go home again. There were five in the Kitchens family and their hired hand, Othal Johnson, seven of us, nine of the Holmeses.

"You don't have room," she said to Aunt Niece. "You can't sleep this many."

Aunt Niece laughed.

"We'll make out. We'll just have to bunk a little closer together. I been wishing all day somebody'd come for Christmas."

The Holmeses stopped their wagon beside ours and the hugging and kissing began all over again, and somebody asked about Uncle Charlie.

"He went to Paris to get Christmas," Aunt Niece said. "Him and Othal. They took a bale o' cotton to sell."

We knew by the way she said it that we could expect a good Christmas.

"You young'uns go watch for him," my grandmother said. "You ought to see him coming up the hill afore long."

We did see him, before dark, a man in a broad-brimmed hat, another man with him, and wagon and mules against a winter sky. He was a tall man and strong, with broad shoulders and straight back. By the time they started up the hill we could tell which was Uncle Charlie, which Othal. When we opened the gate for them, he had pushed his hat to the back of his head, showing his heavy suit of dark brown hair, and was smiling under his wide moustache. At other times I had been afraid of him, but not now, not when he leaned out at us and said, "Christmas Eve Gift."

The wagon had to be unloaded, the boxes and sacks and buckets taken to the kitchen or the smokehouse, the ones he would let us carry. The others got slid under beds, out of sight. Uncle Charlie opened a big package of firecrackers and lined the little packages up on the mantle piece. To us, Christmas was the time for firecrackers, and I had never seen so many outside of a store. He stacked boxes of roman candles beside the firecrackers. He handed Monroe a sack with a pound of loose black powder, and brought in six boxes of shotgun shells.

"I'm aiming to get me some squirrel hunting this Christmas," he said.

He had something else that I saw first in the kitchen—a gallon jug of whiskey which he had set on a shelf with the sugar bowl and some glasses. The men would pour whiskey in a glass, pile in the sugar, and add hot water from the teakettle on the stove.

"Christmas ain't Christmas without a hot toddy," they said to each other.

Aunt Niece, working at the kitchen stove, shook her head. She knew that Uncle Charlie and Othal had sampled the jug on the way home. She did not know how much more sampling they would do before she could set the table for so many.

Neither did my grandmother.

"You gonna make some music after supper?" she asked Uncle Charlie. "Seeing the fiddle box under the bed made me recollect. It's been a whet since I heard any fiddling."

"I might get out the fiddle after supper," Uncle Charlie said.

But he did not. After the first table the men and the bigger boys built up a big fire in the pasture between the house and the front gate. Then, while the women stood on the front porch to watch, Uncle Charlie gave the little children firecrackers and showed how to shoot them. He put a paper fuse against a live coal. When it had lighted it he threw it away from the fire into the dark.

"Don't ever let one go off in your hand," he said. "And don't throw it close to nobody. Somebody might get hurt."

While we went through the firecrackers he had given us, the men made a trip back to the kitchen. This time they brought the jug with them and set it in the back end of a wagon. They brought out more fireworks, and Monroe had the sack of powder in his coat pocket.

"Time for a roman candle," Uncle Charlie said.

He took a long red roman candle and went to the fire.

"You all watch now," he said. "I'm gonna hold it like I was aiming to shoot the gate."

Outside the rim of firelight the night was of a soft, heavy blackness. He lighted the fuse and ran out of sight. We heard a fuzzy pop and a white ball of fire rose and, like a single star, floated through the night, followed by other pops and other stars—red, green, white, red, green, white, enough to take the breath of anyone who had never seen a roman candle. At first he lighted them one at a time, making them last as long as they would. Then he gave one to Othal.

"Let's me and you light up and make out like we're having a battle."

They did, away from the fire, in night so black we could not see them, but we could see the balls of fire, flying straight, stopping when they hit, and dropping to burn out on the ground. The match was even, and they came back to the fire laughing.

Othal stopped close to the blaze to see how to start raveling the string that held together a package of firecrackers. When he did, Uncle Charlie tied a full package to his coattail and set fire to a fuse. At the first pop, Othal whirled toward us. Then he saw what had happened and began running and threshing his hands behind him, but he could not stop the popping. Down through the pasture he went, out of sight, but we knew where he was going by the popping.

Uncle Charlie doubled over, laughing.

"He lit a shuck all right."

Uncle Charlie straightened up and started running, with firecrackers tied to his coattail and popping. Then all the men and bigger boys were running through the night, with firecrackers popping off their backs, in their pockets, in their hands. The smaller children took up the running, without the firecrackers—just running, around and around the house, and through the house, but not in the pasture.

The firecrackers gone, they went back to roman candles, chasing each other, firing at such close range that the smell of powder mingled with the smell of burning cloth. Dewey got a hole in the front of his shirt. There was a smell of singed hair. They kept on running. Into the yard they went, and around the house. Children my size went under the house, behind the blocks of foundation.

On the porch the women were having their say.

"Look out for the door."

"Look out for the bed."

"That'n hit the bed."

45

William

Owens

"They'll burn the house down shore."

With hands and feet they put out the balls of fire that came in the house and on the porch.

Then the roman candles were all gone and the men, out of breath, stopped running. It was quiet, and we came out as far as the yard gate.

Uncle Charlie was not ready for the fun to be over. He went up the steps and across the front porch. Aunt Niece was standing in the door, with the lamplight behind her. He lifted her chin with his finger and went on past her, to the chimney corner where he kept his double-barreled shotgun. Then he came out with the gun under his arm and a box of shells in his hand.

Near the fire, he loaded both barrels and set the stock against his shoulder.

"You aiming at the gate?" Othal asked.

"You got to aim at something."

He fired, and after the blast we heard shot rattle against the gate.

"Got it first shot," Othal said, and ran for his own gun.

In no time at all, five guns were blazing away at the gate, and the little children were running for hiding places under the house. I shivered at the sound, but felt safe, for their backs were to us and they were aiming at the gate.

Then Othal came running around the house, loading and firing as he ran, and some of the others took after him. The women had run inside, but I could hear them telling the men to stop. Too scared to stay under the house, I crawled out and started for the door. In the darkness I ran straight into Othal's knees, and he let a double-barreled blast go off right over my head, leaving a burning flash in my eyes and a ringing in my ears.

"You gonna kill somebody."

The women were saying it first, and then some of the men.

After another round the shooting stopped, the shells all gone.

I got inside to my mother and she held me in her arms till beds for the children had been made down on the floor. Then she put me down and pulled a quilt up over my head.

The next morning the children were up by daylight and out in the yard and pasture, picking up the firecrackers that did not shoot and empty shotgun shells still smelling of burnt powder. We went to look at the gate, and found it half hanging from the posts, with the timbers drilled and splintered by shot.

When we went to the house again the men were at the barn and Aunt Niece was in the kitchen, fixing herself up. She had combed her black hair up all around and piled it in a big knot on top of her head. Her lips and cheeks were pink from pinching. She was smoothing powder on her face with a puff made from real moleskin.

Uncle Charlie came in with a backstick for the fireplace. My grand-mother was waiting for him.

"You ruint the gate," she said.

"I reckon we did."

He laughed, and the light in his blue eyes showed he was not sorry. She frowned and went out to the front porch.

Aunt Niece came in, with a peeled orange in her hand.

"Christmas Gift," he said to her.

She went up to him and stuck a slice of orange between his teeth. They were both laughing without making a sound, and once he leaned over and kissed her.

"I had me some Christmas," he said.

William Owens

The Gulf Oil Can Santa Claus

B
Y THE TIME THE JAPANESE IMPERIAL FORCES WERE DEEP INTO THE mopping-up operations in the Bataan Peninsula, preparations for the siege and fall of Corregidor were also underway. One of the defenders was Clemente García, a twenty-three-year old youngster from Mercedes, Texas, down in the Valley.

He was born not in Mercedes, but in Northern Mexico; his mother, two brothers, and a sister had crossed the Rio Grande at Río Rico, Tamaulipas, Mexico, and settled in Mercedes some two or three years after the death of don Clemente senior who had died during one of the Spanish influenza epidemics that swept Mexico and most of the world, at the end of World War I and well into the Twenties.

Don Clemente had been a veteran of the Mexican Revolution; upon his death, as an enlisted careerist, his widow began to receive a smallish pension from the Mexican government.

Mrs. García's decision to cross the Rio Grande was an economic one and thus no different from the hundreds of thousands of European and other immigrants who settled in the United States. The choice of Mercedes was no accident, however: it was, and remains, an overwhelming Texas Mexican town. Its history and demography reflect that fact, and if not all of the newly arrived Mexican nationals remained there, they did make it a type of half-way house for transients who later spread out all over Texas, the Midwestern United States, and beyond.

These Garcías, then, were merely the newest crop of Garcías to blossom there; to my recollection, there were at least twenty García families in Mercedes. I say "separate" to indicate that these twenty were neither first nor second cousins germane; these were all the main families, and thus the number of affiliated Garcíá families could have numbered fifty units or more. García, however, was not the commonest name, it was merely one of the most popular. As popular, say, as Saldívar or Paredes which are as common as cotton bolls in the month of July.

So, these Garcías settled in Mercedes. Aurora, an only daughter, did needlepoint and constructed some remarkably intricate crepe paper designs to be used as cemetery decorations. Two of the youngsters, Arturo and Medardo, were apprenticed off to neighborhood *panaderías*—bakeries; Arturo to the *El Fénix* and Medardo to *El Porvenir*. Clemente, clearly the brightest according to the family, was enrolled at the all-Texas Mexican neighborhood school: North Ward Elementary.

He logged in the mandatory six years there, and, at sixteen years of age, had learned to read and write enough English to hire on as a sackboy for a local grocery store. Later on, he became the deliveryman as well as the driver.

On his twenty-first birthday, he came to our home and knocked on the east porch door. I was the only one home at the time and invited him in. He thanked me but said that he was in the middle of a delivery; he had stopped, he said, to ask my father's advice on some matter, but that he'd call again.

He was there the same evening after supper. He was typical of many Northern Mexicans, as many of us are, with greenish eyes peering out of fair skin now darkened by a fierce sun.

Our people came to the Valley, as had his, with the Escandón expedition and colonists in 1749; our family happened to live on the northern bank of the Río when it became part of the American Union; his ancestors had lived on the southern bank and thus with the proclamation of the Treaty of Guadalupe Hidalgo, they became Mexican nationals, and we, American citizens.

Later, with the Rio Grande acting as a jurisdictional barrier, the northern and southern bank cultures changed somewhat but not to any marked degree: relatives remained relatives, and *conocidos*—friends-distant-kin-and-acquaintances—were as firm as ever. It was not, then, unusual but rather customary for northern and southern borderers to marry one another. During those times of weddings and other celebrations, the legal crossings of the international bridges were dispensed with; not by the immigration authorities, of course, but certainly by the families and guests involved and then for as long as the wedding parties lasted. The same was true for *pedidas*—betrothals, or baptisms, wakes, and funerals.

Since Clemente had no father, he called on mine for advice; this was in the late Nineteen Thirties and there were still some strong remnants of the old patriarchal system established in 1750. "It's a serious matter, don Manuel," he said to my father.

This was the obligatory phrase and it would encompass almost anything, anything from a request for my father, as a sponsor, to ask for a girl's hand to my father selecting a commission for that same purpose. It could also mean putting in a good word—*dar una recomendación*—on his behalf for whatever was needed; in short, it could be anything, but certainly something of importance to the petitioner.

The Great Depression was still hanging on in the Valley and elsewhere, and steady jobs were hard to come by. For Valleyites jobs were harder still given the Valley-wide agrarian economy which afforded little opportunity. In Clemente's case it was something different: during one of his deliveries in the Anglo Texan side of town, he had met a man named Claude Rodgers. According to Clemente, Mr. Rodgers was going to own and operate a Gulf Oil gas station in the Texas Mexican part of town. And, Mr. Rodgers had asked Clemente if he wanted to work there, full time. Clemente had not known what to say to this, but Mr. Rodgers solved that when he said, "Think it over. Let me know in a week or so."

My father listened to Clemente, nodded, and then pointed to a chair. Clemente sat down, and one of my sisters brought him a tall glass of limeade. I was about to leave them, but my father said I could stay, and I did so.

The upshot was that he took the job; the gas station was directly across the street from our house, and I would see him on a daily basis on my way to and from North Ward Elementary.

In November of 1940, a week before Thanksgiving, as I was crossing North Texas Avenue on my way home, I heard a series of shrill whistles: it was Clemente. "Acá," he said. "Over here." He grinned and yelled out: "Ándale. Come on, hurry it up." He was standing under the car wash which doubled as the car repair section of the garage. It was supported by four solid metal posts, and the sixteen-to-twenty-foot high roof was on a slant.

"What's up?" I asked.

"Look."

"At what? The oil cans?"

"Yeah; I've been saving them."

"Can you sell 'em, like milk bottles?"

He laughed then, and said, "No. I'm going to weld them; all of them. I'm going to weld them and make us a Santa Claus for Christmas."

"Really? Out-a cans?"

"Yeah, you just wait."

"Can I help?"

"You better; it's my Christmas present for you."

"For me?"

"Sure! We'll begin by rinsing and drying them out. What's your dad going to give you?"

"A pair of khaki pants. And a leather belt, from Matamoros."

"And this'll be your third present; everybody's entitled to three, you know."

Thanksgiving came and went, and every afternoon after running errands and doing the daily chores, I'd run over to Rodgers Gulf, rinse some more cans and watch Clemente weld them for the Santa Claus.

"We're going to put it up there, on top of the roof; I'll get me some good, strong wire and nothing'll blow it down; not even the Gulf wind."

That Santa Claus had the biggest belly I'd ever seen; it was matchless in paunch, in roundness, and the black belt was forged out of a series of flattened out cans which gave an even bigger impression of the girth of that old man.

Clemente finished it a week before Christmas, and then in January, on *El Día de los Magos*, the Day of the Magi, or Epiphany as the Church Calendar calls it, he received a notice from the local Selective Service Board.

He took and passed his physical in San Antonio that March of 1941, and he was on his way to the Philippines by October of the same year. What letters he wrote to his mother were brought to my father to read.

Mrs. García, proud but fearful, worried about her two remaining sons. Arturo was found unfit for military service, but Medardo, when he came of age, was drafted and, coincidentally, found himself in the Luzon offensive of 1944; after that campaign, he was sent to Okinawa where he managed to survive the end of the War.

The Santa Claus stayed on top of the car wash for some ten years after World War II. Korea came and went and some of us found ourselves in that "nasty little war" as some correspondent once called it. The Santa finally came down—rusted away, most probably—but due, in greater part, to urban renewal.

In the way of the world of the living, I forgot about it, and I had almost forgotten Clemente García, 'La Norteñita,' as we called him. It was an affectionate name, and a feminine one too. But, he was called that, in the singular, in honor of his favorite song, "Las Norteñitas," "Those Oh-so-sweet Northern Girls."

I had forgotten my Christmas gift from him, as I said, and then, one day, I went down to Mercedes on some now forgotten family business.

Urban renewal had also taken care of the house in which I was born; in its place stood an empty but paved parking lot. Across the street, the old Rodgers Gulf Station had been replaced by a tire store; it was owned by a man named Leopoldo Martínez, a relatively new-comer to Mercedes. (As such he was called a "fuereño," a foreigner, the name usually given to those not born there.)

As I crossed the street to see Martínez, I thought I saw the Gulf Oil Can Santa Claus. I walked on, and I was sure I had seen it again. Somewhere. But how?

I ran inside the store and then almost knocked down a clerk taking inventory.

"Oh, it's you, Doctor. How are you?"

I stopped and looked at him for some sign of recognition but found none.

"I'm sorry," I said. "Who's your father?"

"Leocadio Gavira, the truck driver; he knows you."

I nodded and apologized again. He couldn't help noticing my searching for something and asked, "Can I help you?"

I didn't know what to say, where to begin. Images of the Thirties, Forties, and Fifties flicked on and off and on again as in a slide show until I finally said, "No. . .thanks; I thought I had seen some-thing. . .it's nothing."

He nodded, and as I turned to go, I saw it again; not its reflection this time, but the article itself: a full-blown Michelin Tire Man. The Gavira youngster looked at it, and said, "Oh, that. It's a new line. You know, when some of the older people come in and look at it, they shake their heads. You know why they do that?"

I nodded and started out the door again when he said, "Good to have seen you again, Doctor."

I smiled back and on an impulse asked, "Did you ever know or hear of the Widow García on Hidalgo and First?"

"Sure; she must be ninety, niney-five, a hundred, maybe. She's still alive; lives with a daughter, I think."

And with her memories, too, I added silently.

"Thanks. . .what's your first name?"

"John, sir."

"John! Well, thanks, again."

"Yessir." And he went back to his inventory.

The Michelin Tire Man. It looked grotesque, somehow, but—and again somehow—it looked like my third Christmas present, the one I got the year before the War.

59

*Rolando
Hinojosa-
Smith*

Long Memories

DECEMBER IS AFFABLE. THERE IS A COOL NIP IN THE AIR TO HURRY Christmas shoppers, a few gusts of north wind to blow at the Salvation Army captain ringing his bell, but the days are still bright and clear. It is holiday weather, crisper and drier than football weather, but still two months away from winter.

Hannah is with Eugene constantly now that exams are over and the engagement is official. Tonight it is another eggnog party or an open house, for which she has spent the afternoon sewing a floorlength velvet skirt.

The ironing board is set up in the corner of the dining room by the table which holds our small pile of toys and presents for my youngest sister's children.

"Oh, Mother, it's so exciting I can hardly believe it." Hannah comes in, radiant, in a pink, long-sleeved blouse and a sweetheart-red skirt.

Does she refer to the party they are going to, the new outfit, the way her freshly washed hair fluffs out about her shoulders, or the prospect of Christmas Eve at Aunt Dorothy's? It is hard to tell. Tentatively I respond to my daughter: "You look lovely."

"I mean, he really sounded like he w-wanted to. That it wasn't just something he was thinking he had a responsibility to do."

Oh, yes. *He.* In this case the CPA, her father, my once now all but mercifully forgotten husband Roger.

"Do you think I ought to write and tell him he can stay here?" She is so pleased, so anxious to please.

"Not here. He can go to the rehearsal dinner; Eugene's mother can talk to him. He can come to the reception; the country club under your Aunt Mildred's firm hand can hold both of us. Not here. All right?"

"Well, I can hardly just come right out and tell something like that to Daddy in a letter. Anyway, I'm sure that he will know what is the discreet thing to do." Ever so slightly she raises her chin in defense of her father.

In customary style the CPA has saved his announcement for the back of his yearly Christmas card, which shows all of his new family beaming in front of their large ranch-style house. In similar fashion in other years we learned of his marriage, his move to Arkansas, his sons.

This time he wrote:

> "*. . .will naturally plan to be the one to give away my one and only daughter in marriage. Am sure the young man is to be highly congratulated on his taste. Send me details of my duties when you have them and such extras as the engagement notice from the paper, a formal invitation, and such, so that we can begin to share the festivities in advance.*"

It is so like Roger to appear. He will be trim, graying; his big white hairless body in a well-tailored suit.

We got the news today and I see it is a comfort to her, his promise of fatherhood in February; however much the reminder of him will give me such things as headaches, heartburn, and irritation.

I burn my thumb on the iron as I diligently spread out a blouse of Hannah's. "Tell him whatever you want, honey. We will all be civilized." There must be a reason that people who have lived together once agree to behave in public as circumspectly as the English at tea—probably due to the fact that they no longer remember how it once was. Others of us, divorced, might prefer to remain unpleasant.

"It's so exciting. I can't wait to tell Eugene. It is like a dream come true." She pats at her hair, which in all its thickness, shine, and mass seems to emanate from her very girlhood. (I see it, Hannah's hair, as my annual contribution to the Christmas season.) "You be sure to leave me the gifts to wrap for the kids. You know I love to, and especially Cousin Dottie's, because I want hers to look real grown-up. She's at that age. Do you remember last year how Aunt Dorothy had pink angels and red balls and red ribbons everywhere, and all those branches and holly? It was the most beautiful thing I ever saw. Maybe," she says shyly, "I can do our apartment like that next year. She said some of the angels on the mantle were built around spray cans."

The arrival of the well-groomed Eugene puts a stop to all this. "We won't be late, Mother," Hannah implies a strict and devoted parent.

"Take your time." I burn my thumb again, as, carefully, I apply spray starch to a sleeve.

As she leaves, on her fiancee's arm, Hannah calls back: "Be sure and let us know if we need to pick up your car when we get home."

She smiles from the doorway, framed by happiness and hair. "Maybe next year Eugene will be taking care of your oil leaks for you, Mother."

This blouse of hers seems to have a multitude of sleeves, as when I iron one side of a sleeve and turn it to press the other side, the first side wrinkles again. This blouse is a skybaby blue one that goes with a skirt, and also, well coordinated as her wardrobe is, a pair of plaid pants with cuffs. A heavy metal triangle hot enough to burn flesh seems a poor instrument for readying garments. We should go back, or forward, to washing them on stones in the river and smoothing them to dry in the sun. Soon, a hundred years or so, if we are still here, we can wear paper and recycle it at the plant. This iron will then go in a historical museum. At least it does not have graduated holes which spit steam like the one Mother had.

I am far back in the old days, hearing my mother say "Beverly, you got that dress soaking wet, don't you even know how to use an iron?," when Roy lets himself in.

"Brought us a Lone Star." He displays it as he straddles a chair in the dining room.

"There's some meatloaf left. And Hannah made chocolate cookies." I always offer food to this boyfriend jettisoned in the not too distant past for the unctuous matrimonial Eugene.

"Where's your car?"

"Getting a new hose for what I hope is causing the oil leak."

"Head gasket."

"Don't have any ideas that cost money."

He messes with the bay windows, then remembers that they do not open. He watches me fumble with garments for a while, then says, "Where you getting ready to go?"

"To my sister's, for Christmas."

"You went down there Thanksgiving."

"Other sister. That was Mildred; this is Dorothy. The one who gave the engagement party." To which, naturally, Roy was not invited, but about which he heard a lot over a peanut butter sandwich while he built me a collapsible shelf from which to have my breakfast coffee.

"Oh, her." He thinks about that. "She likes all that family stuff."

"She likes to go to Dorothy's church on Christmas Eve."

"Yeah. Christians are the only ones who can afford Christmas." He shrugs as if it didn't matter. "She taking her sweet-boy along?"

"They're saving that for next year."

"Types like that aren't in a hurry for anything."

There is a blouse that looks like heavy satin with a tie at the neck that must be to wear to church. I know from experience that these things Hannah sews are, however, mostly synthetics and need a very cool iron. With some relief I negotiate it, and get it safely on a hanger.

"Let's go get the car." Roy is restless. "You never rode in my new car, did you?"

"No." But I do remember a good ride in his old car. What a nice car that was. I borrowed it once, on our old street, and was entranced with the smell of grease, plastic, and stale cigarettes, very fragrant. It reminded me of cars in Sally that I never got to ride in, cars with missing hubcaps, busted radiators, dented fenders, the kind that showed steady use. Where the back seat was, in Roy's old car, was a gaping trough with two or three jacks, an old spare, a few untouched schoolbooks, a disintegrating blanket, a paperback porno, and a wool sweater his mother must have searched for everywhere.

His new blue Mustang revs up its rpms and takes us down the street, giving a very smooth ride. My hair is still damp, as I do not get it fancy for Dorothy, and the wind whips it about my face. There is something about the clean vinyl seats, the radio blaring away, and the manner in which Roy keeps adjusting the rear-view mirror that reminds me of double-dating. All that is missing is the cherry Cokes.

At the second stop light a lot of cars honk at each other, hands wave out the windows. The kids, paired and packed in, look as though they are on their way to park, bumper to bumper, on some dark hill overlooking the lake. Group necking.

"Creeps." Roy speeds past them. They are not his crowd, or rather, he is not their crowd. It can't be by choice that he is running errands with Hannah's mother on the first night of the holidays.

I try to cheer him up. "You're driving like we were in a stock-car race."

"You scared?" He doesn't mind that.

"I think they're cops behind every tree."

He takes a sharp curve. "When girls do that," he says, as I hug the door handle, "I reach across like I was gonna open the door and say, 'You wanta walk?' That usually puts an end to that."

Impressed, I take my hand away and roll with the turns.

At the service station my plain vanilla Plymouth is waiting in the row of finished cars. There is no dark stain seeping onto the concrete beneath it, at least. Cars have so many ways of getting to you.

"Hop out," Roy says, swinging open my door across me. "I'll meet you back at your house."

"You don't need to."

"I didn't get my chocolate cookies."

Roy and his life remind me of my days of trying to make it out of Sally, Texas, population 5280: One Square mile of Friendly People.

When I think of the town itself, and not about my family in particular, it is easy to get the homesickness and the nostalgia that you feel for those imaginary places, like rolling blackland farms with pigs, that you invent for your past. To my memory, nowhere else on earth is as flat as outside Sally where the edges of the horizon in all directions wave into a steamy watery mirage that reflects the grasshoppers pumping oil and the old wood farmhouses and the fields of new green sorghum shoots.

My sisters and I had the good do-nothing times in Sally that are a large part of the life of any small town—fooling around after school along the railroad tracks, jumping from tie to tie, racing to the nearest crossing; there was the game of putting your ear to the steel rail to hear if a train was coming. One time we climbed into an empty boxcar and switched dresses. It was a very daring adventure, to be where we had no business being, stripped down to our panties.

Sally bloomed twice, once when they brought in the railroad and again when the oil company began to produce in the fields to the north. All the buildings in town are distinguishable as railroad landmarks or as new modern oil improvements. When the oil money came in and the company town was built, Daddy moved his drugstore to a new building across from the Church of Christ, the drygoods store put up new awnings, and the town installed its first parking meter.

In its heyday, Daddy's drugstore was a social gathering place for men from in and around town. He liked to listen to his old friends, farmers, who came to town to talk about the threat of downy mildew to the grain sorghum and the advisibility of trying Fasgro 131 and the idea of caterpillar control through using papernest wasps, and what the going price of anhydrous ammonia was. That kind of talk was about the life he had moved to town and gone into the drug business and helped send Chester, his younger brother, to pharmacy school to get away from. He liked to be reminded of his escape. Such conversations assured him that he would never have to watch his crops being plowed under, as his dad had. Besides, as the men said, it was no use to work your back bent growing crops, when your neighbor like as not was going to buy a Piper Cub with the oil leases on his back forty.

His ears ever open to word of trouble, Daddy was one of the first to say that the oil was going to peter out and he was leaving before it did. Which, with all of us in college and gone, he did. He took his nest egg and the secretary-treasurer of the Ladies' Auxilary to the Volunteer Fire Department, and moved to the metropolis of Corpus Christi, away from the daily ag news about the county agent and the migrant worker and failing town. Mother didn't mind the move: because things are lush and green in Corpus and visitors from home oh and ah over the seacoast, and she has her sister who married well to tell about the success of her daughters Mildred and Dorothy, and how even Beverly, the least likely, is holding her own.

Roy and I give up on the ironing. With our window open over the table-shelf, we get a strong dark December wind, which blows the last moisture from my hair. It smells almost like frost. (Surely the right sort of night for going down a rocky mountain path to Bethlehem. Once in Sally they had a live creche at the Lutheran church with loose chickens and sheep wandering around and an old jersey cow who made a patty by the straw. A nice pregnant farm girl was Mary. It was the most believable Christmas I can remember.)

Roy watches as I comb out the tangles. "I quit school," he says.

"What happened?"

"Nothing new. I was busting out anyway. What was the point of making an F plus just for coming to class."

"What did your mother say?"

"Mom screamed at me for an hour that I'm as good as dead without an education. Then she called community college and told them they'd better not drop me if they knew what was good for them. Then she followed me around half the night to prove that I had plenty of time to study if I wanted to. As I did, instead of finishing off the six-pack. She won't get the idea that I don't want to. I can figure out what they're talking about in there; but I can't figure out *why*."

"What did you tell her?"

"I promised I'd start over in the fall if she'd get off my back. She tells me at least once a day, no school, no future."

It is easy to understand his mother: if you have been kept down, if your husband was kept down for not having schooling, you've got your eyes on thirty years from now because you are still thinking of thirty years back when.

"What do you want to do?" I ask him.

"Saturday night?"

"With your life."

"You mean how do I want to make money. That's what you types always mean." He sees that I'm like his mom, and gets the rest of it off his chest. "It's different for your daughter. All a good-looking girl has to do is get married. She could bust every course and it wouldn't matter a damn."

"That only puts the problem off, getting married."

"Yeah, you tried that, didn't you?"

"So did your mother."

"I said good-looking."

I let it go and asked the question he wants to hear instead: "What do you want to do Saturday night?"

"Ball, what else?"

I smile, not able to fault that. We give in and eat the last of Hannah's cookies and add our trash to the growing stack.

"Be seeing you," he says.

"Thanks for taking me to get the car."

"What do *you* want to do Saturday night?" he asks, from the back door, his jacket zipped up.

"Ball, what else?" I smile to use his word.

"Oh, *Mother*—" Hannah and Eugene stand, shocked, in the doorway to the dining room.

"Long time no see," Roy sticks out his hand.

Hannah is miserable, her cheeks white, her eyes full of tears.

"You're the one who drives around campus looking for us, aren't you?" Eugene confronts the unwanted guest. He has the air of a boy who has seen a dog run over and stops his car to remove it from the street and rings doorbells to try to find its owner. He didn't hit the dog; but he isn't evading his responsibility.

"Must be someone else," Roy says, slouching against the door. "I've got better things to do."

"You d-did so, Roy," Hannah accuses. "You drove past the fountain again last week and kept honking and staring at us. You know you did."

"Must have been someone else. I'm got other things to do. Your mother and I were just talking about what else we got to do."

Hannah turns scarlet with shame and lifts her hand to strike his face. She is innocence, brought to this in her very own home.

Eugene, still in his coat, shows Roy the door. "When we're married," he vows, "this will never happen again."

After Eugene has gone, Hannah lets herself cry. "Oh, Mother, how

61

Shelby
Hearon

could you? How could you let a person like that come around?"

"Roy isn't a criminal element. He fixed this shelf, this table for me, remember? And the fence around the garbage cans? Who else saw that I was without a place to put my elbows and read the paper, who else cared that my pantry overflowed with trash? Who around here deals with me about reality? He's a boy you used to date, Hannah."

"He has embarassed me so bad I can never face Eugene again. And you honestly don't see anything wrong, do you?"

"I think he wanted to talk to you again. You represent something to him, something he had lost."

"Roy never had any part of me, Mother." Her face is red and angry.

"He's dropped out of school and his mom is upset."

"You let him come here and eat lunch, too, don't you?"

"He is welcome to eat a peanut butter sandwich. Why not? You keep up with former husbands of mine."

"Oh, Mother, that isn't the same at all, writing to Daddy, and you know it." She goes into the dining room to wipe her eyes and pull herself together. I see her going through the stack of unironed clothes. In a very tight voice she says: "I'll finish pressing up these things you didn't do, Mother, if you'll do the dishes. We'll have to wrap Aunt Dorothy's presents early in the morning." Wordlessly she sprinkles and begins to iron her nice clean holiday clothes.

It isn't Sally, Texas, Hannah reminds me of, far from it. Rather it is the once-resident CPA: noting some matter that I have mishandled, pointing out some unacceptable behavior that I have just lapsed into. His words float over Hannah's flocculent hair, ghosts, like the over-voice on a TV commercial, telling me that once again I have flunked out of propriety the same way Roy flunked out of school.

"Eugene knows it isn't your fault."

"You didn't even notice." Tears run down her face as she shows me the long-awaited symbol of her betrothal. "He gave me my r-ring."

There is the diamond of splendid caratage that Eugene has placed in a proper setting on her long white finger. He presented it, she tells me, in his formal front room (while I was letting my hair blow dry in a blue Mustang), in the presence of his mother, who wanted to share in the surprise. It was given tonight so she would have it to take to the traditional close family gathering around Aunt Dorothy's pink and ruby Christmas tree. ("This is the last holiday we will ever spend apart, darling," Eugene surely said, as he sealed it with a kiss.)

"How can I ever look him in the face again?"

"You can, that's how. He will forget the whole thing." I take her some tea.

"I won't." Hannah's wet eyes look at me reproachfully. "I never will."

And I see that my daughter takes after me in one way at least: she neither forgives nor forgets.

63

Shelby
Hearon

Drawing by BARBARA WHITEHEAD

Christmas Past

WE HAD ABOUT 20 TO OUR HOUSE THAT TIME. THE BIRD WE cooked was 25 pounds or more. There were Umpie Zack and Uncle Shirley and their wives from Louisiana, my wife's aunt and sister, and Uncle Shirley's and Deed's kids, one of whom was my student now, and of course M.H. and Ronnie B. were here, and their boy, and our younger girl. Our big girl was off this time in California with her husband's family; but my mother and my mother-in-law, the Queen Mother, were with us, and my sister and her husband and boys, and our friend "Uncle" Roscoe, the Curmudgeon; and our special guests were Judge Joshua and his wife, both our friends, and her Dutch mother, well into her 80s and pretty as a Brueghel.

The magic of Christmas comes, I think, in a kind of trinity like old Dickens's fable of Christmas past, present and future. There is the magic of the Eve, and of its meaning, whatever your personal belief or faith may be; and of the morning, the giving and receiving, that special feeling that we privileged children of the world have known, and of the shared bounty of the board; and then there is that other magic, which may come these days or yield to television, that bridge back to the "real" or secular or whatever world you want to call it, whatever we do to complete the ritual and reassure each other that the time, its significance and meaning, will come around for us again.

However that may be, we'd sat together at two long tables, one making a T to the other from the dining room into the livingroom, and I at the T-head, and after blessing and toasts we'd had the turkey, cranberry dressing, sweet potato pudding, asparagus, beans, rolls, as on the dinner rolled, and then the boiled custard or the steamed plum pudding and sauce from Uncle Roscoe's curmudgeonly kitchen. Judge Joshua, with dedicated help from nearly everybody else, had led the way with gracious and spirited toasts fore and aft, with French white wine and then with Spanish champagne with the dessert.

After dinner and a partial dispersion, those of us remaining hunkered for a moment together, standing and sitting, stretching and yawning, at the end of the livingroom. The Judge allowed he would indeed have a small balloon of Spanish brandy, into which folly Roscoe and I followed him. He looked red of face and happy, hair a bit unruly, vital as life itself with his laugh and smile, so happily and cleverly disguising the damaged working of his shredded heart. My chief need is to recall him, now, in his happiness and vitality, for his departure was an unbelievable shock, even knowing what we knew. I wish to say that, living, Aaron Joshua meant whole orders of knowledge and experience to me.

Uncle Shirley declared he would stick with the bubbly. The red fire licking at the oak and locust in the fireplace was too hot, was ridiculous in fact, for the snow that had gently come down on the prairie to bless the Eve was melting or melted now. It was warm outside, with grass yet green under snow and the sky as blue as forever and the sun crinkling up the afternoon edge of Christmas day.

My wife said that those of us who wished to smoke might go out on the deck, overlooking the back yard. Most of us repaired out there, smokers or no. I had reserved some big cigars for the day and Ronnie B. at least helped me indulge in them. Roscoe smoked his Larks. Judge Joshua had eschewed all such, but he tied into that brandy. The air was clear; the sun warm; the breeze blew the smoke in wisps. Now the story telling could begin.

One of the kids asked Uncle Shirley to tell his story about stopping at some tents at the roadside and eating barbecue, thinking it was a carnival or something, and trying to find the man to pay, and being ushered in and asked how much stock he had in the company; or his story of his friend Prejean calling him from Cajun country in south Louisiana and asking how many kids he had, and Uncle Shirley telling him three, and asking how many kids Prejean had, and Prejean saying five, and naming them off over the phone and naming four, and then saying, "Oh hell, man, I ain't got but four!"

"I think you have just told it," Uncle Shirley said, offering to do one of his famous card tricks instead. Everybody booed. We all knew that the main reason we had been sent outside was so that he would not do his famous pick-a-card trick where he throws the whole deck at the wall and your card sticks up on the wall with a thumbtack through it, leaving holes.

"Uncle" Roscoe, who taught Shakespeare, declared that he never told stories, either as jokes or experiences, and considered it a low art form. He urged the assembled younger people to go this moment and read something to improve their minds, like *The Tempest*. We voted him a brick for his efforts, which he immediately used to clout young Michael up 'side the head.

My mother then declared that Dickens's *A Christmas Carol* had been a favorite of her mother's, and I remembered her, my grandmother, fierce-eyed, white-haired kinswoman of Anne Hathaway, telling me so, and in that moment got a perfect picture of her, alive and talking to me, that took my breath away and made me feel very young again. My mother suggested her son bring out the book and read us some: "Oh! But he was a tight-fisted hand at the grindstone, Scrooge! a squeezing, wrenching, grasping, scraping, clutching, covetous, old sinner!" Even though I had control of the supply of beer, wine and brandy this idea was also booed.

"Ah! But what a wonderful terrible pitiful old skinless heartflint he was!" I declared.

"Are those your words or Dickens's?" the Curmudgeon asked.

Undaunted, I persisted in mentioning Christmas Past, Present and Yet to Come: the times of childhood, of youth and maturity, those times when opportunities for love and humanness were real, and often lost, the times before our hearts and minds became set in the patterns that now characterize us: the too-seldom reclaimed moments of joy in life.

Aaron Joshua remarked that in us all were memories of sad and happy, good and bitter Christmases. He said he loved the song "Hard Candy Christmas" from *Best Little Whorehouse in Texas* and would be happy to render it for us. His wife, Vanyna, said she would never forgive him if he did. "These ones coming along can't sing so good," said her mother, who had come up in the church in Holland, where singing mattered.

Then Umpie Zack and his wife and my wife's mother joined us on the deck. Umpie Zack had fortified himself with a dollop of Old Charter, ice and lemon. The Queen Mother sat, for a moment the sun kindled to a blaze off of her jewelry, her regal form serene, her eyes the depth of the purple-blue of the Aegean. She had submitted to the knife and denied the damnable demon four times in nearly 20 years. In mind and body she, more consciously than most of us, fought mortality.

Umpie Zack sat with his bourbon, handsome in his 70s, ring flashing on his finger, keen of eye, Roman of nose, for all the world the governor of Louisiana, the Caesar, the ringmaster for whom we were awaiting to build the ritual.

"I could tell about Christmas at the mill when we were girls," the Queen Mother said. "It was just a small mill town, with the roaring furnaces. . ."

I looked at my mother, and saw an image of my father, and all of us around our tree, growing up there in Ohio, where sometimes the snow would come and we would go into the snowy woods, the woods of Old Man Zeke Demar who had built his log house there nearly 100 years before, and cut the tree, by his permission. . . .

But Umpie Zack had thought of something, and began to tell it, something from a time back in their Louisiana town.

"We had some hard times in that little town," he said, "back in the early 1920s, and then again the Thirties, the Depression years. At my store there then we used to put on shows, you see, to attract the customers. Once we had an Ape Man who cavorted in the window. But I was left with the ape suit, had to buy the damn thing.

"One time a man came in and said he would be the Automatic or Mechanical Man in the window for $25. His act was to get all made up and lurch and lunge around, turning his head real jerky like a machine and doing his arms like this, three times a day. He would stand up there in the window with this wire in his rear like he was working on electricity and then offer $25 to anybody that could make him laugh. Old Hilda, a mammy, nearly did break him up, though I never knew what she said to him.

"But the best act was the Hypnotized Lady. I guess she really must have been hypnotized. She would sleep in the window of the store, advertising the bed and a Beautyrest mattress, for two days and two nights. The man came in the store and offered me the act and I said, 'Well now, sir, how does she relieve herself?' He said not to worry about that.

"She would sleep in a negligee, you know, from Carpenter's Department Store and have a sign saying 'Madame X's Coiffure is by Miss Bonnie's Shoppe' and so on. Everybody would get a piece of it, but she was at our store, and those old boys would come in from the country and gawk and say, 'I believe she's daid,' or 'She's a wax dummy.' 'Nah, you can see she's breathing.' You could too. She was a *good*-looking woman too.

"Then at the end of two days and nights, they'd wake her up and interview her, and she would put on this act and wake up fluttering her eyes and feeling her head and say, 'Where am I? Am I in Atlantic City?' But she would lie still all that time and never toss or turn or anything. And there would be people still staring in that dark window after I turned off the lights and started home at eleven p.m. . . ."

Umpie Zack stopped and shook his head at the memory.

"What does that have to do with Christmas?" someone said.

But Umpie Zack did not answer. He was just getting started.

"Another thing we used to do," he said, "to advertise at the store was to have a salesman who was a great baker come down from Chicago every fall to bake biscuits on a wood-burning Majestic range—"

"I hope this doesn't mean that you all are getting hungry again so soon," my wife said. "It couldn't possibly, could it?"

I walked our Cocker out into the yard to sniff the grass and the few patches left the of snow. Judge Joshua came along with me.

"Good story," I said.

He smiled, his frontiersman's face happy and his lawyer's eyes full of the peace of the moment and the humor and mystery of the Mechanical Man and the Hypnotized Lady. "Good Christmas," he said.

We looked back at the porch where the ones we loved sat and then we looked up at the burnished evening sky.

"Moments, Jesus, moments," I said.

Aaron Joshua took a long deep breath, and let it out.

"Ah Christ!" he said.

69

Marshall Terry

Star of Hope

ALL CHRISTMAS EVE THE BROTHER AND SISTER TOOK TURNS WALKING the sister's tiny baby up and down the room while their own youngish parents commiserated. There seemed to be no consolation for the suffering child. He showed no interest in the twinkling Christmas tree, but why should he, since he was only a month old and in pain. "Poor little infant, new to this world, had to meet his very first Christmas in suffering," its mother said. "It's so sad for a baby to be sick on this blessed night when another baby long ago was born in health and joy." The forlorn grandfather shook his head and murmured, "Right here at Christmas."

By early Christmas morning, the baby's condition was grave. When the doctor came he sent the family at once with the gasping infant to Methodist Hospital. There they were told that the baby was stricken with spinal meningitis, a disease fatal to almost anyone and certainly to an infant one month old. There was no money. The sister's husband—eighteen like his wife—had disappeared when his young wife had told him she was going to have a baby. He was a moody loner from the western Texas mesas, a sort of sullen cowboy. When he vanished, the sister came home. Her father, a poor salesman, said, "I don't know what we're going to do."

"Just depend on the providing of the Lord," her mother said. "As we always have."

"I'll just have to see if I can borrow some more from the Company," he answered. "And right here at Christmas."

All Christmastime the family—mother, father, sister and brother—sat silently together in the corridor of the hospital outside the baby's room. The tree at home, abandoned, was unlighted and the presents were unopened. Earlier, in the years before, there had been different Christmases.

There were candles on the tree and cotton for snow, and a piece of almost-magic, a star cut out of cardboard and covered with tinfoil by the mother, slightly crooked because she couldn't get the points even. It shone down from the treetop: A Star of Hope. This handmade piece of splendor lay all year swaddled in cotton in a shoebox in a high, dark shelf in the mother's closet. Each year the brother and sister attended the ceremony of the descent of the shoebox from its safe preserve. They witnessed their young mother wavering on a chair in the closet, her head lost in the dark heights, straining with sighs toward the shoebox. Down it came, triumphantly reclaimed one year more from the dark reaches as the mother proclaimed, exulting and perspiring, almost as if she had pulled the star from the very sky, "Well, here's our old star."

Early Christmas morning the young father would be up before it was light and he would light the small gas heater— a stranger in this tropical climate, set alight only on festive occasions, as if it were a part of the fireworks—whose asbestos cones glowed orange with heat by the time the others got there. The room was already too hot. But the brother and sister clutched at the stockings filled with an apple, an orange, some nuts, some Christmas candy sticky from the heat, fireworks: A Roman candle, some sparklers which they ignited at the gas stove and showered in the room. Golden candlelight, silver sparkler light, orange gas glow, the blue starlight that the precious crooked star cast down upon them—this was the family's Christmas morning light in the days before.

71

William
Goyen

As the day advanced it got hotter and the gas stove was turned off and the brother and sister went out into the humid Gulf Coast morning to roll their toys and pull their wagons. Once they saw a boy— not one of their favorites—come down the street on a tiny Shetland pony. They paused to watch as he rode grandly by. "He was standing by the Christmas tree," the boy called out. My mama and daddy brought him in the house and tied him to the piano."

"What's going to be his name?" the brother and sister cried.

"Christmas—what do you think?" the boy answered, and went on.

It would be so hot by mid-morning, and already the unnameable sadness of Christmas had fallen upon everybody. "Wonder why?" the son asked his mother.

"To remind us that we are mortal and must struggle," she answered—an answer that was no clarification for the boy then. Later, when he was sixteen, he thought he knew a glimmer of what his mother meant; and much later, when he was thirty, he was sure he knew.

By noon the family's street was alive with Texas people. Kinfolks, all dressed up, were arriving from neighboring towns with food and presents and jumping children. Front doors and all the windows in houses were open and the radios were blaring a mixture of Christmas carols and hillbilly music. From their house the Light Crust Dough-boys from Tennessee, brought to Texas radio listeners by Bewley's Best Flour, were singing their noon program, which the mother listened to. Firecrackers were going off here and yonder. The sun blazed down and electric fans were on.

The family had to dress up for Christmas dinner, eaten in the afternoon. The grandfather came with whiskey on his breath. That rankled the mother. Later she would draw the father, whose breath now, too, had the smell, gotten from his own father's hip pocket where a half pint always travelled with him, onto the sleeping porch and tell him that he would have to take his father (who had walked twenty blocks from a cheap mission hotel in town) back if he drank anymore. "Hell, Lou, it's Christmas," the father would protest, almost apologetically. There was a muffled argument that finally soared into clear, final words from the mother: "And you can just go with him. Then you all can drink all you want to on Congress Avenue."

The son went shyly in to see about his father and saw him sitting on the side of his bed, looking down at the floor. He had often seen him this way.

"What's the matter, Daddy?" he softly asked the gentle man who always seemed so tired.

"Nothing, Son."

"Then come on out with the rest of us," the son said.

"You go on, Daddy'll be there in a minute. Go on, now. But Son, let me tell you something. You be good to your mama, you hear? Because she went through the shadows of the valley of death for you, to bring you into this world."

When these words were said to him by his father, they made him so sad that he would go off by himself for a time. There was some large sadness in the world, made up of disappointment and some unnameable unhappiness, that the boy kept feeling, more and more.

Other kinfolks arrived, all trouble for the mother, all her mortal enemies—the father's city family. Hers remained in the little town she grieved for, a shady, pineywoods place on the banks of a soft river. She often cried at night to go back there. "That's alright," the son heard her tell his father as he lay in his bed in the next room, so close it was as if they were all in the same bed together. "One day I'll just take the children and go back home. You can stay here with your folks in this infernal city. That's what you want anyway, to live under their coat-tails while they drink and run around."

"But Lou, the company moved me here. We had to come. The sawmill's shut down—you know that."

"You could have gone back to the tailor shop. Jack Moody said he'd take you back."

By this time the sister and brother had been moved into separate beds, a parting that they could not understand. The sister, then twelve, had been removed to the front bedroom. Every night after the parents were surely asleep, she crept back into her old childhood bed with her brother. "I'm scared," she would whisper.

The father's three citified sisters, not a one of them with a current husband, were wearing Christmas regalia. Two of them had on dresses—red and white—of starched cotton, hard as boards. The young one, May, a Texas pathfinder of fashion, wore green slacks. Though the father always protected his young, wild sister, he had little patience with her, still in her twenties and already married twice and her second husband long gone. The mother had no patience with May at all, and at the sight of the tight slacks, her face turned hot red.

"A lot of the women are wearing them at the sewing factory," May informed everybody. "Keeps the men from looking up you all the time. Ha! Besides, they're comfortable and real keen to wear. Lou, you ought to try you a pair."

The grandfather, May's father, said, "May, that's not right. A man might as well get himself another man if a woman's going to wear pants. Don't see much difference. But 'course none of my children ever listen to me, so go on, wear what you want to, can wear the Lone Star flag don't make any difference to me. I'm old and going to die one of these days in the Hope Mission on Congress Avenue."

Everybody was quietened by this outpouring from a habitually silent old man. Guilt and sorrow beyond expression lay over the family for a moment. And then the father murmured, "And right here at Christmas," and shook his head and made the sound of "Whew!", a sound of renunciation, the way he did.

Now Christmas dinner filled the table. The rush was on the mashed sweet potatoes covered with toasted marshmellows and the Texas gravy, simmering in a boat of wonders—livers and hearts and giblets and boiled eggs. Ice cream had already been made and the freezer was packed with wet newspaper over salt crystals to keep the cream from

73

William
Goyen

melting; and the big white coconut cakes were set out on a separate table where they seemed as innocent and fresh as brides. Joy, no matter what strife unsettled the family, rose blithely out of strife and moved through the members, not understanding and misunderstood, and they ate together in some kind of love, born where they did not know, and in simple unquestioned reunion.

In the darkness of the hospital room, where only a dim lamp shone, the family could see, when the nurse opened the door for a moment, the child, descendant of its Texas generations, heir to Christmases and crises of love and loss and crooked hope, lying motionless under a canopy of gauze in a white crib, struggling to stay, to be joined to this family, these generations. Despite all its hopes and prayers for him, this family might have bitterly wondered, being tired and worn of hope and confused with one another—*why?*

"My little baby," the young mother said. "And I can't even hold him."

"You'd think his daddy might come back to sit by his own little son's sickbed," the mother told her. "Not to mention sending the little thing a Christmas present."

The young mother said nothing, only cried softly. And then she said wanly, "But how would he know?"

Day after day, night after night, the little family sat outside the door. "I've done all I can," the doctor told them. "Only God is keeping the little baby alive. Pray."

The family prayed outside the door of the mysterious room where the baby, now four months old, struggled, with only strangers' hands, nurses' and doctors', to touch it, no bloodkin's touch, no mother's warmth. The mother said now that she would never know the feel of an infant. "Even if the baby comes out of that room alive, I'll never have known what it was to nurse a little baby. I've lost my baby, either way."

The baby kept on living, a day at a time. Hope glimmered, against all medical discouragement. The father had lost his sales job after wrecking the company car on the highway; it was reported that he had whiskey on his breath. The grandfather had found his peace— overdue—on a cot one early morning in Hope Mission. May had run off with a sailor and was heard from in Norfolk, Virginia; the baby's boy father, the runaway cowboy husband, had stayed out somewhere in a hiding place and still had not been heard from. But though loss and fear and even death touched his kin outside in the roiling world

74

William Goyen

beyond his dark room, the baby, beyond human help, breathed and struggled and held onto his life. He was six months old.

And then one morning in late March, near Eastertime, when the family got up to go to the hospital, they saw snow falling. Snow! White, blessed snow was sprinkling on the ground and over the green trees in the back yard, turning it into a place the family had never seen. The mulberry treestump had icing on it like a cake.

"The first thing I thought was that I wished the baby could see the snow," the sister—the baby's mother—said. "And then suddenly I knew that the baby was going to Heaven. God's sent the snow to show us that." It really seemed that way, what the sister said, and the others felt it without saying anything.

It was the first snow the sister and brother had ever seen. Their parents remembered a few times of it back home. "Once three inches of it fell," the mother remembered. "Chickens and geese were befuddled and cattle huddled together in the white fields, lowing like it was the end of the world. Some said it twas. We nearly all froze to death, cows and chickens too."

In the small city of Houston that March morning, sleds appeared out of nowhere; who had sleds in Houston? People threw mushy snowballs, some tasted of the stuff, others were afraid to go out in it. Some church bells rang and schools closed. But within a few hours it was as if it had only rained. Still, there had been the transforming vision of the snowfall.

And the baby died. One day in June, when the snow had long since melted and gone, a nurse moved from the shadows of the room and stood solemnly at the door of what had seemed like a tomb. "It's like he's really just been born," the mother said. "Into the hands of the Lord who will take care of him where none of us down here below knew how to."

"Well, I guess he has a chance this time," the sister told them all. "He's been just a memory to me for so long, even on some days like a make-believe baby; I couldn't get the feeling of holding him, he passed through my arms so fast way back there at Christmas. I see now that he'd been taken from me a long time ago. I've been just looking through a door at a ghost baby in the dark, a stranger to me." The brother held his sister while she sobbed deeply for the first time; almost, it seemed, in liberation from the bondage of a ghostly motherhood.

The family got in the car together and went silently home. In the front room they saw for the first time in all these months the Christmas tree. The presents were there; the tree was brown and dry, but stalwart. In a while it was the mother who climbed the ladder and lifted from the tree's brittle crest the star and brought it down. She put it, one more time, in the shoebox and silently went to the back room to lift it up once again to the dark shelf of the closet.

76

William
Goyen

Celebration

Geese break on the sky
          in eddies and drifts
         pour past the horizon
           in luminous waves:
             dissolving, reforming
            the rites of the morning.
               Four hundred and more
                  in organic rhythm
                      pound the air thin—
                  dropping goose music
               pierced by the silence:
             measure the silver
          of sun on a wing:
          transmigrate the unmarked
           fathoms of azure,
        the unceasing currents
      pulsing the compass:
          erratically stitch
        the earth
to its season.

Jacqueline
Simon

Safeway Logs

Yes, I have used
those pressed-sawdust fakes
that promise:
"The ROMANCE Without the HEARTACHES"—
and true, they catch with just a match.
But though their fire burns evenly
no sparks drift up
like winter thoughts—
catherine-wheels, burning gold,
then cold, then ash.
No star-exploding resins crack
drying or dying in the wood;
no fragmentary promises are charred
within that pyre
with which to make
another fire.

Christmas and the North Pole

S ANTA CLAUS WAS THE FIRST PERSON TO SEE THE NORTH POLE. HISTORY
might not have recorded this, but Thomas Nast did.

Eighteen years before the end of the nineteenth century, when
no man or woman known to civilization could claim having been in
the vicinity of Ninety Degrees North Latitude, Nast depicted Santa
sitting atop a mail box labeled, "Christmas Box 1882, St. Nicholas,
North Pole."

Nast's cartoon seems also to represent the first time anyone desig-
nated Santa Claus' residence as the North Pole. The cartoonist left no
explanation for choosing the top of the world as Santa's residence, but
the warm dress traditionally worn by the fat man no doubt had much
to do with giving him a very cold habitat.

Other theories had been voiced much earlier about the polar climate. A few men of supposed education and intelligence had in ages
past speculated that the golden apples of the Garden of the Hesperi-
des would be found growing at the North Pole, that the site of the
Garden of Eden was in that location, even that Plato's lost Atlantis
was there, instead of near the Strait of Gibraltar. As late as the onset
of the twentieth century a few scientists, or maybe they were psuedo-
scientists, speculated that the North Pole lay on a land rich in mineral
resources. Others, obviously a bit more enlightened, believed an ice-
free northern sea would be found surrounding it.

No one knew for certain. No one had been there. Humankind actually knew as much about the moon, some of which was at least
visible.

The identity of the human being who was first to reach the North
Pole is still a matter of speculation and even, in limited quarters, bitter
controversy, but I believe that the man, Robert Peary, generally credited with the attainment, did indeed get there first. In the early 1960's I
researched thousands of items in his personal papers—then in the
possession of his daughter, Marie Peary Stafford of Brunswick,
Maine—for a biography that was published in 1967.

One Christmas after that, when the season's-greetings mania
grabbed me for some reason, I mailed a capsule account of Peary's life

79

John
Edward
Weems

to a limited number of relatives in Texas and friends throughout the United States who I thought might be interested in the subject. Here is the capsule biography, with the wish that it may be of some interest to you this holiday season, in Texas or wherever you are.

"I must have fame," young Robert Edwin Peary told his mother more than once. In the dwindling nineteenth century, large areas of the planet still had not been visited by man. After much deliberation, Peary made his choice: he would become an arctic explorer, would be the first man to reach the North Pole.

If his initial reason for wanting to become a renowned explorer would seem wrong later to many people, he did have a logical defense. Some persons of close association tended to look down on him and his mother because of their economic status. His reaction to this resulted in an obsession to excel somehow.

Peary could be called a self-made man in the truest sense. Within three years of his birth on May 6, 1856, at Cresson, Pennsylvania, his father died. His mother packed family possessions and took her "Bertie" and Charles Peary's body back to her native Maine. There she buried her husband, established residence, and devoted herself to bringing up "Bertie"—almost as a girl. Mary Wiley Peary taught him the handiwork practiced by genteel young ladies of that period and sent him out to play wearing a bonnet to protect his fair skin. Nearly as dismaying to this sensitive boy was the fact that he and his mother (who never remarried) were considered poor relations by the family. All this propelled him at an early age to prove himself. Significantly, his youthful companions soon used "Bert" as his nickname.

Peary graduated from Portland High School, earned a degree from Bowdoin College, then took a naval commission in the Civil Engineer Corps with the thought that work on a proposed Nicaraguan canal might win him fame such as had come to the Frenchman De Lesseps for the Suez Canal. Nicaraguan plans collapsed, but Peary stayed in the Navy.

About 1885, Peary's interest in the North was rekindled. He began poring over voluminous reports of arctic explorers during his free hours. On October 13 of that year he wrote himself a memorandum (which I found in 1962 in his own voluminous papers) that the time had come "for an entire change in the expeditionary organization of Arctic research." Instead of utilizing large parties and several ships, he wrote, he would have a small group relying on Eskimo assistance. He had not been to the Arctic then, but the method he outlined would eventually bring him success.

From 1886 to 1909 Peary devoted himself to planning and leading eight arctic expeditions—one of them of four years duration. With increasing difficulty, he obtained leaves of absence from the Navy, raised his own money, recruited his own men, made his own rules—and expected strict compliance.

During one expedition, he froze his feet and lost most of his toes to amputation, then suffered hellish agony when frequent bumps against jagged ice left the stumps bloody and aching. Nevertheless, arctic exploration continued to come before all else: health, the Navy, finances, family (he married Josephine Diebitsch in 1888; they had two children).

The early desire for fame became an obsession to reach a goal. During years of exploration, Peary mapped unknown lands and showed Greenland to be an island, but he did not get to the North Pole. To him this meant failure.

Finally, he succeeded, at the age of 52—a wiry, auburn-haired, mustached man who could still hold his six-foot frame erect, but whose drawn, ruddy face and squinting eyes indicated hard experience. On April 1, 1909, he said good-bye to the last of four compact supporting parties that had accompanied him across the treacherous, evershifting ice of the Arctic Ocean. Then, with a black assistant, Matthew Henson, four Eskimos, five sledges, and 40 dogs, he struggled across more floating ice and reached the Pole five days later, according to his navigation, only to return to civilization and learn that Dr. Frederick A. Cook, a former Peary expedition member, was claiming to have arrived first. Virtually all scientific and geographical organizations eventually credited Peary with the achievement and discredited Cook, but controversy still flares occasionally.

In recent years, some authors using computers on Peary's published navigational records have sought to prove he never could have covered the distances claimed. But in 1959, when I was researching an earlier book on Peary (with emphasis on the Cook controversy) Vilhjalmur Stefansson, the foremost arctic authority of his time, the last of the dog-team explorers, and no particular worshiper of Peary, told me, "Most of the arctic men find the Peary mileages reasonable. I could have made them. Many others could have made them. . .under the circumstances given."

After 1911, Peary retired as a rear admiral, voted the "Thanks of Congress." For nearly a decade he and his family enjoyed normal life, although the Cook dispute cast a pall. On February 20, 1920, Peary died from pernicious anemia. His self-acquired Christmas present, the

81

John
Edward
Weems

polar attainment, never did prove to be the golden reward he felt that he had earned.

Letters of condolence and tribute came from presidents, kings, geographers, and explorers. It was Peary himself, however, who had expressed the most appropriate tribute—years earlier. After the polar attainment a college classmate recalled that Peary had an affinity for quoting some poignant lines written by another Bowdoin man, Henry Wadsworth Longfellow:

"A boy's will is the wind's will,

"And the thoughts of youth are long, long thoughts."

82

John
Edward
Weems

A Christmas Collage

MY CHRISTMASES ARE CUMULATIVE. SINCE OURS WAS A CONSERVAtive family, with a thrifty Dutch father who came off a Yankee farm in central Illinois, gifts represented love and warmth but were seldom profuse. My father's family had always given him and his siblings presents of nuts and fruits, concentrating instead on the holiness of the season. Although my mother bent my dad forward somewhat, both of them were inclined to give us what we needed as the year unfolded and seldom saved anything back for Christmas.

Growing up in Texas, of course, I never saw a white Christmas until I was 58 years old, and that was in Munich, Germany, not in Texas. One Christmas when I was about 12 my cousin Kincaid and I doffed our shoes and went tadpole hunting in 90-degree weather. We were going to nurse the tads into frogs, but Kincaid made the mistake of leaving the tadpole bucket where Grandpa Buckley could find it. He threw out its contents like so much garbage, thereby ruining our chance to become frog kings of Parker County and ending my short career in entrepreneurship at the dreaming stage. I have been a salaried minion ever since.

I grew up a painfully shy introverted kid who gradually forced himself out of the shyness but never overcame the introversion. My father and sisters were doers, while my mother always described herself as "reserved," which was her way of refusing to extend herself in any direction. I was more like her, except once when I was about seven years old I had to walk in front of the church congregation at Sunday services to receive a certification that I had been promoted from beginner's Sunday school to advanced beginner. I remember the incident painfully, for I had been given new shoes for the occasion. Naturally they squeaked, as all new shoes for boys did in those days, and I lumbered with my back in the shape of a question mark and my head between my knees like a sheep-killing dog.

My mother, who wanted to be proud of me and had come on that particular Sunday so that she could be, took me straight out of church and lectured me in her quiet, no-rebuttal way. She let me know that I had made a shameful spectacle of myself, and that I must always bear myself proudly and look everyone in the eye. I forced myself to do better, but it required effort until I was at least in my late teens. In the anonymity of the classroom I could be a terror, snapping my fingers and interrupting and smarting off, but to get up in front of people, never.

This hang-dog self-effacement even carried over to my parents. Once they went off to Kansas for several days to attend my brother's college graduation—he was 19 years older than I and no factor in my life until I was an adult, after which we became the closest of friends. When Mother and Dad returned, I hid behind the skirts of Florence, who had been keeping us while they traveled "up north," and refused to greet my mother for maybe three days. Meanwhile my outgoing sisters were jumping all over both parents and hugging and kissing like mad, thereby making my behavior look all the more reprehensible. I still fight that tendency, and after I have been away from my colleagues in the Department of History at The University of Texas for a protracted period, I will delay as long as possible before returning to my office and taking a chance on seeing someone I know and would like to see. If I had been Caesar or Napoleon, I would never have returned from a year's triumph heading a magnificent procession. Instead, I would have sneaked in by rowboat sometime after midnight.

Or as one long-time administrative assistant used to chide me, "Why don't you ever come home friendly like other people?"

I bring this up for one reason. I hated Christmas get-togethers in which anyone was present whom I didn't see regularly. The first Christmas I remember was held down at Grandpa Buckley's at 1810 South Main Street, where the road divides to the Harmony community on the right and to Spring Creek on the left. (It's been replaced by a modern Church of Christ now, which I consider a black mark against that denomination, since Grandpa's was my favorite of all the places I ever played at.) I was probably three years old, or maybe four. My cousin Kincaid received a rocking horse. He was a month older and seemed to have been born two inches taller and 10 pounds heavier than I and held that position through life. I looked up to him as an elder statesman. Lately though, the month's seniority doesn't seem to matter.

I don't remember what I got, for I was psychologically blanked. We all gathered in the front parlor, with an old black leather davenport which made down into a bed. Our family gatherings were always festive and hurt my ears. But Santa Claus, bless his heart, came and started "ho-ho-hoing." I was entranced. Then my cousin Kincaid, who you must remember was a month older and therefore a month more sophisticated than I, said, "That's not really Santa Claus—that's Uncle Johnny!" Now Uncle Johnny was possibly my favorite uncle, along with Uncle Willie, Uncle Frank, Uncle Louie, and Uncle Milton. But Kincaid's revelation that Uncle Johnny was playing a false role hit me so hard that I funked out. I studied my knees, folded one over the other; I buried my face in my too-big sweater; I wouldn't look at the spurious Santa Claus or the jolly Uncle Johnny. It was the most miserable Christmas of my life.

'Til the next one. And the next one.

I do remember that I gave Grandmother, whom I adored unreservedly, a big bag of jelly beans. That was 15 years at least before I had ever heard of Ronald Reagan, whose presence I first encountered as the Gipper.

Except for my mother my family were superb at oohing and ahhing over gifts. I would try, and the words would stick in my throat. If I really liked a gift, I tended to go off and cry. I cried when I received my first watch, and I cried when I received my first bicycle. I will probably cry when I see the flowers on my casket. Who says the dead don't cry?

Nowadays they would have passed me to the school counselor who would have lateralled me on to the local psychiatrist. Then I would have turned normal and have nothing to write about.

Once we had a big Christmas festivity at the old Baptist Tabernacle in Weatherford. This time it may have been the real Santa Claus that showed up. At least I didn't have my discerning cousin Kincaid beside me to tell me that Santa wasn't genuine. This Santa handed out bags of fruit and nuts and candy kisses to all the kids present. By name. When he called out mine, I wouldn't go forward. He called again. One of my sisters half rose in her seat to get the bag for me, at which Santa spotted me and came down the aisle to hand the package to me personally. I was man enough to reach out for it.

Since we weren't Baptists, I can't tell you why we were present at a Baptist Christmas party, except that maybe, being full of Dutch acquisitive acumen, we didn't want to pass up any freebies—or even more likely, my oldest sister may have been currently romancing the church's choir director, a recurring event that made ecumenicists out of us before any one in Weatherford had ever heard of the term.

My favorite Christmases occurred in Fort Worth, where I lived

85

Joe B. Frantz

across the street from Adrian Womack, whose uncle, a former liquor wholesaler forced by Prohibition into the Buick agency, indulged him the way favorite uncles with few nephews are supposed to. (My own family was so crowded with cousins that no uncle could have afforded to indulge one of us.) Every Christmas Adrian received what seemed to me fabulous gifts—football outfits, a pool table, baseball gear, a horse. We were in our sports phase. I felt no jealousy toward Adrian, as he was generous in sharing use of his gifts with me. Not that I was neglected. Not at all. I received my share of footballs and baseballs and bats and gloves, though never in the profusion that Adrian did, since my parents were sharing with five kids and Uncle Womack was giving his all to only one boy.

Seasons didn't matter. All sports were in season, and I have hacked away at baseballs and golf balls on Christmas day, in 40-degree weather, as though it were springtime in Florida. We played with our gifts until they truly wore out, after which Adrian and I would get our cord and his Grandma's heavy needles and sew the covers back on the balls. When the balls were beyond resewing, we would cover them with tire tape. I got so that I could hit a black ball better than a white one.

The females in the family seem to have originated division of labor. Mother never had to tell any of my sisters what to do nor nag at them like many mothers do. At Christmas, each had her cooking specialty. Mother made the pies, unless it was chocolate with meringue, in which case Ruby baked it. Nellie cooked 50 pounds of fudge, pregnant with pecans. Josephine stuck to basics. We all ate like voracious dogs for three weeks or so. In those days I was unbelievably skinny, as contrasted with my pear shape of today—44 pounds at 8 years old, 80 pounds at 13, 105 pounds when I finished high school, 125 pounds when I married in my early 20s. I ate—nay, I gorged—with impunity. The whole family did, and no one ballooned. Apparently I ran mine off with my scooter and my sports gear, and the remainder of my family received its share of exercise reaching for the next portion.

Through it all, my mother barely touched the food, although she loved to cook. Each Christmas I would buy her a box of chocolate-covered cherries, Renfro's special at 49 cents, which in an era when most kids seldom saw cash fit my budget; and she would react as if I had brought her linens from Ireland. I don't know how many successive years I gave her the chocolate cherries, but I followed the conservative sports maxim religiously: never change a winning combination.

Besides, she would always share several with me.

So at Christmas time we would eat turkey and mashed potatoes and sweet potatoes and English peas, hot biscuits, gravy and cornbread dressing with lots of onions; plus six kinds of dessert, usually with second helpings, after which we would repair to the living room to finish off the meal with chocolate fudge and divinity, though the latter never held much appeal for me. Dad would open a huge package of "red hots," not the weiners but a kind of stingy mint or jelly bean, and he and I would try to demolish them. By every chair was a plate of nuts, pecans mostly but also walnuts and almonds, and we would work on them. Why I didn't blow a gasket in my body I'll never fathom, but I survived.

Then Adrian would show up with his plunder from Uncle Womack, and he and I would move to the out-of-doors to run and wrestle until the back of my head would pound.

Ours was a musical family, although I lagged badly. All three sisters played the piano, and we would sing popular songs until Dad joined us, after which we would sing Christmas hymns until Dad left for his nap or until his early bedtime. Mother seldom joined the singing, preferring to sit in the next room and listen or read or just wait for the spring seed catalogs to arrive. She loved to sing, but only when she was alone—or thought she was—in the house, when she would chord the keys and try to reach A above high C. We children felt she nursed a frustration to be a professional singer, but had been discouraged by Grandpa Buckley, who looked on almost anything but farm work and its accompaniment as "foolin' around." He also had three sons who nurtured the dreams of playing professional baseball and indeed received some overtures, but that too came under the heading of foolin' around. Still another one of his daughters wanted to either sing or paint, and being the youngest and the most petted, dared to take lessons in both branches of the arts but only after she was married. Mother just waited till she thought the house was empty and then opened her vocal chords. Sometimes we surprised her with our presence, and she would look embarrassed. So we sang without her at Christmas.

As I said at the beginning, my Christmases are cumulative, and the rest of this rambling reminiscence will show how. Eventually my marriage produced two daughters, which led to a reenactment of previous Christmases, except that now I was the parent. Without getting sentimental, I shall never receive greater pleasure than when Helen and I hit the target with certain Christmas presents for the children. I recall once giving Jolie a present, and her looking at me and saying in a 5-

year-old's voice redolent with wonder, "Is this really for me? You mean it's mine?" I felt then the power of Christmas, the pleasure of bringing pleasure. You can give great gifts—furs and Mercedes and trips to Monaco, none of which I have ever given—but when you give a child the present that hits the spot, then a material Joy to the World turns spiritual, and your soul soars. But only children can transmit that special moment, for they don't worry that you paid too much or that you bought the wrong brand. They receive, and their eyes light. I am fortunate in having two daughters, Jolie and Lisa, who knew how to inflame my heart.

One other Christmas still stands out. I had been overseas in the Pacific for a year when my destroyer was ordered home for an overhaul just a few days before Christmas. We headed into Puget Sound, with Seattle and Bremerton as twin destinations. As so often happens in winter in that part of the country, the area was shrouded in fog. We couldn't see the gunwales on the ship unless we were leaning against them. A pilot came aboard 20 miles out of Seattle to guide us in. With his musician's ear he could identify every sound that came to us from other ships and navigational aides. It was, to use a cliche, eerie. Supernatural. Nothing seen, only directionless sound.

Suddenly a new sound intruded—from above, from the water, from the port, from starboard, from stern, from forward. "It's heavenly music," said Soper, my signalman, who I thought knew only four-letter words. Another man whispered reverently, "Listen, it's angels!"

It might as well as been. We could see neither shore, nor anything between. Yet sound enveloped us. Undoubtedly some sailor on some nearby unseen shore had turned up recordings of Christmas carols to the decibels usually associated with today's rock and roll. But the fog filtered and spread the music until it inhabited us, and we tired sailors, who hadn't seen America for a year, all broke down and cried. For a moment USS *Wilkes* (DD 441) became a shrine. Sailors whose recent aim had been to survive for the next spree experienced a rare moment of holiness. We had heard the majesty and the meaning of Christmas.

88

Joe B.
Frantz

Christmas on the Jigger Y

I DO NOT REMEMBER WHEN I FIRST BECAME AWARE THAT THE ANIMALS on the ranch paid the same attention to Christmas that they paid to Sundays. That is probably the main reason Christmas always seemed more an ordeal than a celebration to my father. It disrupted an ordered and necessary routine.

Four of us Kelton boys grew up on the McElroy Ranch east of Crane, Texas, in the edge of Upton County. Known as the Jigger Y, from its brand, it was a big outfit, about two hundred and twenty sections as we reckoned it then, almost a hundred and fifty thousand acres as people tend to figure it now. It sounds like more than it was, unless you were riding across it a-horseback. In Crane and Upton counties it took a lot of acres—fifty or more—to keep a cow's ribs from showing like a washboard. It was the kind of country a real-estate man described to me in graphic terms many years later: "Sorry as hell, but pretty good."

The ranch had been put together at the turn of the century by El Paso rancher-packer J.T. McElroy out of part of the old open-range Quien Sabe outfit. When we lived there, though, it belonged to a French-and-American syndicate which had bought it in 1926 for the oil that lay beneath its sparse grass. To us, the owners were "the Frenchmen," a mysterious group who showed up every couple of years from somewhere beyond the ocean, dressed to the nines and speaking a language that made us wonder how they knew what they were talking about.

Though their main interest was oil, the cattle operation was expected to stand on its own. That was the responsibility of Fount Armstrong, the original foreman who hired my father in 1929 as a cowboy, and it became my father's when Mr. Armstrong left to pursue his own ranching interests after a couple of years and Dad became the foreman. One way and another, Dad saw to it that the cattle operation lost money only a couple of years out of the thirty-six that he remained on the ranch.

One way was by getting the most out of every working day, and that is why Dad was never enthusiastic about Christmas as the rest of us were. Whatever the livestock needed on the twentieth of December, they needed just as much on Christmas Day. The difference was that Dad had plenty of help on the twentieth.

Mother's and Dad's conception of a proper Christmas holiday was basically different. Mother had grown up in a farming and ranching home where Christmas was observed with a trip to church, with family singing of hymns and carols, with a tree and a lot of trimmings, colorful even though not expensive. Dad, on the other hand, grew up in a Spartan ranch atmosphere more than twenty miles north of Midland, far from a church, far from any type of organized Christmas activity. In a country later to grow up with a heavy infestation of mesquites, trees of any kind were scarce in his boyhood. Not even a cedar could be found for a Christmas tree.

To Dad, we had just as well have brought a wagon or even a cow into the house.

In his time and place, it was customary for schools and churches to set up large community-type trees, but it was not general custom to have an individual family tree in the home. My mother theorizes that one reason for Dad's lack of enthusiam might have been an incident at old Florey, a now-forgotten community near Andrews, when they were first married. The church had a large Christmas tree and Christmas Eve program at which presents were to be exchanged. Mother's two youngest sisters, Ruth and Christine, were small girls at the time. Dad went ahead of them, hiding under his coat two wrapped packages containing dolls. A large crowd watched him set them under the tree. One of the dolls gave out a loud "Mama!", and the crowd roared, at Dad's expense. He retreated red-faced to the back of the building and thereafter avoided both churches and Christmas trees for many years.

The ranch tended to be almost deserted for two or three days at Christmas. It was not really *home* for anyone except us kids. To all the adults, *home* was somewhere else because no one there had lived on the place for more than a few years.

In those days, most of the working cowboys tended to be either "young" bachelors or "old" bachelors. I don't remember anybody ever being considered a middleaged bachelor. He was young until he got to be about thirty, then was evidently considered beyond marital redemption and automatically was classed as "old," at least in matrimonial terms. Ranches generally in those days seemed to have little or no provision for married cowboys except those of foreman status, or those who might hold down an outlying camp that had suitable living

Drawing by BARBARA WHITEHEAD

quarters. Bachelor cowboys at the McElroy lived in an L-shaped bunkhouse building which provided small individual rooms, not the dormitory style of living which the term "bunkhouse" implied. Most of these cowboys had some better place to be at Christmas, and as a rule they went.

Most of our growing-up years, we were the only children on the place. Lester S.Grant, a mining engineer from Colorado, managed the ranch in addition to the company's local oil interests. The Grants' sons were grown and never lived a day on the place. Cliff Newland was the ranch's windmill man. The Newlands' daughter and son stayed with a grandmother in Midland so they could attend a bigger school than Crane's. That left it to us four Kelton boys to entertain ourselves the best—or worst—way we could.

We looked forward to Christmas partly because it gave us a wider variety of playmates, cousins we seldom saw. We spent a big percentage of our Christmases at the ranch of our paternal grandparents north of Midland. To us the old couple were always Daddoo and Mammaw. Bill Kelton—Daddoo—had been a working cowboy since he was about twelve, a necessity brought about by the early death of his father on a family homestead in Callahan County. As the oldest of four sons and two daughters, he had to help make a living for the family. He broke horses and mules and worked cattle for various ranches in the Baird area, later cowboying from the lower end of the Pecos River to as far north as the XIT. When my own father was about five years old, times became tough in Callahan County. My great-uncle, Frank Kelton, wrote home that cowboy jobs were to be had at Pecos. My granddad made up his mind to move his family. Grandmother had seen Pecos, however. She vowed that they would not move one mile farther west than Midland. Granddad insisted they were going to Pecos.

At Midland, he got a job first as a drayman, then as a cowboy north of town. He spent fifteen years as foreman on the Scharbauer Five Wells Ranch before acquiring a ranch of his own in partnership with Arnold Scharbauer. It was on that ranch, the Hackamore N north of Midland, that we spent many a happy Christmas.

It was always a great family get-together—uncles, aunts, cousins —in what seemed to me a delightfully pioneer setting. At the McElroy we had all the modern conveniences—indoor plumbing and electric lights from a thirty-two-volt Delco system. Daddoo and Mammaw still had kerosene lamps, and a trip to the bathroom was a short walk in the backyard to a small wooden structure which at

Christmastime was likely to freeze any bared extremities. It made you save up until necessity was no longer to be denied.

The ranchhouse was a small, simple old box-and-strip structure put up about the turn of the century. My grandparents' bedroom still had the original "wallpaper," old newspapers dated about 1903 or 1904, complete with color comics of Buster Brown and other early strips already extinct and exotic by the 1930s. One of the delights of any trip to that ranch was a chance to reread the old "funnies."

A couple of years ago I revisited that place when the old house was finally being dismantled. I looked in vain for any sign of those ancient comics.

Heat at Christmastime came from two sources, the cookstove in the narrow kitchen and a big pot-bellied heater standing in the living room. The walls were thin and only a modest barrier to the north wind, so we stayed as near that heater as possible, freezing one side while we roasted the other. The old house had a small attic room which Daddoo for some reason called the "chute." A set of outside stairs led to it. When extra cowhands were needed, that was their sleeping place, the ceiling so low they could not stand up. At Christmastime we visiting boys slept on pallets in the chute, close to the warm chimney that came up from beneath.

The toys we received were small by today's standards. A dollar bill seemed as big as a saddleblanket in those Depression days and was not lightly spent. But our expectations were not high, either, so we took grand pleasure out of whatever we did receive. Always of a bookish nature myself, I was never in greater glory than when I received a couple of fifteen-cent Big Little Books, especially the movie-story kind that featured stills from a Ken Maynard or Buck Jones Western.

The big fun of Christmas was in playing with cousins George, Daisy and Ruby Gilbert, or aunt Clarabelle Kelton, the baby of her family and in about the same age bracket as the rest of us. We played hide-and-seek, ring-around-the-rosy and spin-the-bottle. If weather was too bad for us to go outside, and we had plenty of time for a stretched-out game, we played Monopoly. We were never aware that the material side of Christmas might be a little short; nobody in our circle of acquaintances was any better-off. The greatest gift of that season was enjoyment of family.

Sometimes Daddoo let one or two of us to go with him to feed his cattle. He never owned a pickup to the last day he lived on that ranch. He had a car, but ranch work was done a-horseback or with a wagon and team. He kept "cow cake" in a big old sheet-metal structure we called the red barn, though it was red mainly from rust rather than paint. The cake was forty-one percent protein, made of cottonseed, and had a rather pleasant taste if you didn't chew hard and grind your teeth on the grit. Daddoo had a plank loading dock built just wagon high so he could drag out the hundred-pound sacks and drop them into the wagonbed. Under his wagonseat was a wooden box which he filled from the sacks. He carried along a small scoop, and as the cattle came to his call he gave each a single scoop of cake.

At least a couple of times we went with him to gather dead mesquite for the two wood-burning stoves. On one occasion which came to have grave significance to me in later years, a front wheel of the wagon dropped into a hole, and a big stick of wood fell, striking Daddoo on the back of his neck. He had a black birthmark there, about the size of a quarter. He doubled over in pain, which surprised and scared me. I was too young to realize the birthmark was melanoma, already giving him trouble. It would eventually kill him.

The wood-gathering ventures may have ended with my brother Myrle, three years younger than I was. Daddoo gave him the responsibility of holding the reins—from the ground, of course—while the rest of us gathered wood. Something spooked the team, which jerked the reins from Myrle's small hands. They stampeded back to the house, hubbing a gatepost as they wheeled into the yard. The wagon was rendered into firewood along with the dead mesquite.

A highlight of Christmas at the Hackamore N was dinner on Christmas day. Our grandmother always had turkeys behind net wire which enclosed perhaps an acre north of the house. A grass or weed seedling had no chance; those turkeys kept that ground as slick as a peeled stone. One of them always made the supreme sacrifice at Christmastime as the centerpiece of a well-stocked table. Everybody who came brought cake, pie, fruit salad and the like, so there was never any shortage of good things to eat, only a frustrating limitation on our ability to sample everything. Even Mammaw's red beans were special. During the long years Daddoo had been a ranch foreman, it had been her duty to feed ranchhands in whatever number there might be on any given day, from one or two to a dozen or two. Above all else, a ranch cook had to know how to fix red beans.

The worst thing about Christmas was that sometime soon after dinner we had to load up the car and start home. We faced a trip of about seventy-five or eighty miles, the first third of it over two-rut roads treacherous with high centers and, when it rained, bottomless mudholes that could quickly undo whatever religious feelings the holiday might have fostered. It was hard to maintain the Christmas glow through that tiresome trip, especially if all the ranch chores were waiting for us when we got home. Dad usually had some in mind.

Christmases at home, on the Jigger Y, never seemed to have quite the gaiety of those trips to the Hackamore N, even when the same kinfolks showed up. The change of scenery was probably the big difference, plus the fact that what was an outing at Daddoo's and Mammaw's, like hauling wood or feeding cattle, was simply a chore at home, especially if we were doing more than usual to make up for the holiday absence of the other ranch people.

At home, or at our grandparents', Christmas was always simple and unstructured, the gifts modest in cost and few in number even though rich in spirit. I don't think I was ever prouder of any Christmas gift than of a "cowboy suit" when I was seven or eight years old. Mother made me a pair of brown chaps out of some type of oilcloth, which at night with the light behind me might have passed for leather. I probably received a cap pistol to go with it, but it is the chaps I remember. I already had the boots. In fact, I never wore shoes until I was far along in grade school and gradually learned that, away from horse and cow work, boots are for vanity and shoes are for feet.

What toys we received were sturdy and usually lasted a long time. We made or improvised much of what we had. On the south side of the house, weather permitting, we played with miniature corrals made by punching matchsticks and twigs down into the sand. Marbles were our cattle and horses. We used them this way far more than we ever "shot" marbles in the accepted manner. In a time when real cattle tended to be either Hereford red-and-white or Angus black, we had "cattle" of all colors in which a marble could be found. That was either a throwback to the days of the spotted Longhorns or a prognostication of today's exotic crosses which produce herds of a rainbow hue.

Our improvisation might have been appreciated by Dad, who was saving every possible nickel to pay out his personal herd of cows bought on credit in 1928, just *before* the crash, but it was not always appreciated by others on the ranch.

Seldom were we in grander style than when a grocery trip yielded us a cardboard carton large enough to hold one of us boys while the others pushed him around over the gravel-covered yard. The gravel helped keep the box moving smartly, but it produced a sound akin to that made by a piece of chalk scratching down a blackboard. That was a particular nuisance to the manager, Mr. Grant, and to Mrs. Grant, a city woman who hated every day she spent on the ranch and avoided all contact with us Kelton boys except to stop us periodically in the yard and search us for matches.

One Christmas, just before leaving for his annual holiday trip to his original home in Colorado, Mr. Grant gave us boys a bright red Jumbo wagon, presented with a smile and an expressed hope that never again would we push each other across the yard in a cardboard box.

Christmas is by its nature a family time, and Tom Schreiner had no family to observe it with. He had been divorced long years earlier, but divorce was a thing discussed in whispers, so we considered him an old bachelor. He had come from Norway in his youth to make his fortune in America but wound up keeping books for others while they made *their* fortunes. His own somehow always eluded him, despite his having personally hand-delivered the multi-million-dollar check by which the syndicate had bought the huge old Jigger Y from J.T. McElroy. He lived on the ranch as its resident bookkeeper for many years, supposedly exiled from the oil company's main offices because of his propensity for drinking.

His broad knowledge and persistent accent added a cosmopolitan flavor to our fence-bound lives. He had seen much of the world. He had a patient understanding of the foibles of men. . .and boys.

He had a few foibles of his own, chief of them a penchant for periodically staying too long at the bar in town. It often amused us at the time, but now I realize he must have had many dark frustrations to drown. He had come from a spectacular land of towering mountains and deep blue fjords and had led a colorful early life in such diverse cities as New York and New Orleans. It must have been a bitter disappointment to spend his "harvest years" on what surely seemed a drab and colorless outpost long on dust and short on scenery.

Tom Schreiner stories are legion among the Crane oldtimers who knew him. I remember the late Sunday afternoon when he came walking in along the town road, looking for Dad to help him. He explained that he had run his coupe into a ditch a mile or so short of headquarters. At the time he had five cans of cold beer left. Ever an accountant, he mentally calculated how far each beer would have to last for him to come out even.

"And, Buck," he said with justifiable pride, "I just missed it by a hundred yards."

Christmas must have been a lonely time for him, for though he was part of the ranch's extended family he remained always basically a loner, pacing the long porch of the company office or the short porch of the little company house which had been allotted him. He shared only peripherally in the various family observances. For the most part he sat in his little house and drank alone. If we saw him at all during the holidays, we were usually a little embarrassed for him.

I remember the Christmas one of us boys, or perhaps all of us together, received a basketball. We were dribbling it across the packed earth of the big yard when Tom Schreiner came out, a little unsteadily, to watch us. He decided after a time to join the fun. Taking the basketball in hand, he kicked it a considerable distance, falling in the process. He told us, "Venn I vass a young man, I vass very good at *base*ball."

That poor basketball was one plaything which did not last us long. It landed in the cultivated cactus patch by the office and exploded like a balloon.

All the years we knew him, Mr. Schreiner talked lovingly of the "old country." It was his dream, upon retirement, to go home and spend his final years among family and boyhood friends. At last, old and ill, he returned to Norway after World War II with his pension and whatever savings he had accumulated. Sadly, nothing was as he remembered it. His relatives did not know him. The friends of his youth were aged or dead. Even the face of the land had changed. He was more alone there than on the ranch. He wrote melancholy letters about his plans to return to Texas as soon as his health improved.

It never did. He died, as alone as ever, in the old country of which he had dreamed so long. In the end, even his dreams abandoned him.

Christmas was not always a happy occasion for all of *us*, either. I went with Mother once to the funeral of a young cousin the day before Christmas Eve. That same Christmas, my brother Bill held onto a "baby giant" firecracker and split his thumb. Bill was always accident-prone, most of his troubles having to do with horses. When he was just a baby, Myrle and I were bouncing him in a canvas seat suspended from the ceiling. The spring came looose and hit him on the head, nearly killing him. When he was old enough to walk, he exercised that ability too near a horse's hind feet and was kicked in the stomach, which again almost killed him. Later on he hung a foot in a stirrup and was dragged almost to the point of death.

Our youngest brother, Gene, nicknamed Boob for the old comic-strip character Boob McNutt, almost had a fatal accident one frigid Christmas. He waded out onto the ice which had formed across a big surface tank at the ranch, and he fell through. Myrle broke ice all the way out from the edge to save him. When they got back to the house, their wet clothes frozen stiff, Myrle got a spanking for letting Boob go on the ice in the first place. Virtue was always rewarded, but not always as expected.

For us kids, the elation of Christmas was always followed by a letdown as life all too quickly returned to routine. But Dad always seemed glad when it was over. He was of the old school of stockmen whose priorities were to see first to the horses, then to the cattle, and finally to one's self. He mellowed a great deal in later years, when his grandchildren came along, and seemed finally to enjoy Christmas vicariously, through them, in a way he never could through us when he was a young man heavily burdened by responsibilities that sometimes seemed impossible to carry.

I never realized how informal and unstructured our ranch holidays were until a Christmas I spent as a soldier in Austria in 1945, in the home of the young woman who was to become my wife. There, old customs were deeply ingrained, and an elaborate ritual was played out a step at a time. For more than thirty years afterward, every December brought the same comment from Ann: "Somehow it doesn't seem like Christmas." With some misgivings, I took her back to Austria for the Christmas of 1981, half afraid she would be disappointed, that her memory had played her false or that times would have diminished the ritual. The fear was for nothing. It was not just the way she remembered it; it was even better. Each generation had preserved the customs from the preceding ones and added a bit more, from the attendance of Christmas Eve mass to the lighting of candles over relatives' graves in the cemetery, to the singing of carols and reciting of prayers at home, the lighting of the Christmas tree candles and finally—for the long-suffering children—the signal to start passing out presents.

I thought I could better understand Tom Schreiner's annual Christmas melancholy.

But one thing in the Austrian Christmas was the same as in the ones we had on the Jigger Y or the Hackamore N: the warmth and sharing of a family love that never had to be put into words. It glowed as brightly as would the Christmas trees we never had.

The Night Old Santa Claus Came

(This is a true account, as faithful as memory can make it after more than fifty years. The mama referred to is Mrs. Ruth Capps Martin, who now lives at Nederland, Texas. She was a pioneer in one-teacher schools, later became a pioneer in Special Education in Texas public schools. After many years, through many vicissitudes, she did indeed further her education, taking two college degrees.)

IMAGINE A WHITE SCHOOLHOUSE SITTING ON A HILL. IT HAD TWO LARGE rooms. The one on the north was full of desks, blackboards, a bookshelf, a teacher's desk, a pedal organ, and everything needed for the seventeen pupils who attended Mama's school. It smelled like chalk dust and ink and glue.

The other room in the schoolhouse was ours. It was the only place at Anarene for us to live, but it was a good home. It had a kitchen and closet curtained off at one end, with a kerosene cook stove and linoleum on the floor; the rest of our room had a lumber floor and two beds, one for me and Bill, one for Mama and Roy, and in between our wood-burning heater stove.

Roy was five years old. I was going on eight. Bill was nine. Mama was ancient, at least thirty, maybe even thirty-one. The pupils who came were different ages, two in highschool, two in the first grade, the rest scattered in between. They walked in across the prairie and through the mesquite brush from every direction each school morning. From schoolhouse hill you could only see where four other families lived; the other kids had long walks, and one rode horseback.

At one end of the white painted schoolhouse rose a flagpole, where we flew the U.S. flag on good days; at the other end stood the cistern with its squeaky pully and fuzzy rope to draw drinking water. Out on the flat ground we had three swings and a see-saw, a baseball field to play scrub, a garage for Mama's Model-T, and the woodpile and toilets. From schoolhouse hill you could see a long way, and it looked lonely out there—not much happening, except a few white-face cattle grazing.

That winter Mama said she hoped it would snow at the right time so we would have a white Christmas, but we would take whatever God sent. He did not often send the best snow to West Texas, but usually north wind and blowing sleet.

Mama was rich. Since she was the principal as well as the teacher and also mopped the schoolhouse floor, she got paid a hundred dollars a month. They had said when we first came there that you could not be a teacher at Anarene unless you could whip the biggest boy in school. They did not know her; she had fierce eyes. She was beautiful, but she could look at a big boy and say, "I thought you were older and more responsible than that," and he would start blushing and stammering.

But usually she gave rewards. If a big girl made ninety on spelling, Mama would let her sit in one of the long desks and teach a smaller kid his reading lesson. Or if a big boy did good in Geography, Mama would let him bring in wood or stoke the fire or draw water for the water keg.

We had been thinking about Christmas and one Saturday Mama gave me and Bill and Roy each fifty cents for gift money. We could spend it any way we wanted to, but Mama said, "Remember, it's better to give than to receive." Even more exciting, we were going shopping that day to the great city of Wichita Falls. She needed to buy some bright crepe paper and things for decorations. She did not ask the school trustees about such things, but used her own money because she made such a big salary.

Mama knew how to get to Wichita Falls and all the streets and stores, for she went up there sometimes to junior college. She had got her certificate that showed she was smart enough to teach school a long time ago by taking a test at the capitol of Archer County. But she said that in her spare time she might as well further her education. So she got assignments from Wichita Falls and did them at night after us kids went to bed and sent them in through the mail. Anyway, me and Bill and Roy found ourselves in the biggest nickel and dime store in the world with fifty cents in our pockets.

Everything looked bright and colorful and shiny, hundreds of things in trays and hanging up where ever you looked. And the store smelled good. I could have walked around in there for weeks just looking.

Roy was dumb. He could not see past his own nose. We were not supposed to spy on what each other bought, but I could not take care of him and not let him get lost without seeing what he did. And here's exactly what he did. He bought himself a thirty-five-cent wind-up caterpillar tractor made out of tin with rubber tracks. Then he lost a dime and never could find it. The last nickel he spent for a sack of yellow candy corn, which he stuffed down before he even got back to the car. Me and Bill told him how dumb he was and said, "Boy, you're going to be sorry when it comes time to put gifts on the Christmas tree." It didn't seem to bother him, but we said, "You wait and see!"

I got Mama a new spatula to turn pancakes and Bill got her a handkerchief with flowers embroidered in the corner. I got the other two kids a pewter whistle with a bird on top; you could put a little water in it and it would make a tweeting sound. But I didn't know whether I wanted to give Roy a present or not; a kid of five ought to be more responsible than that.

The school days got long during the week before Christmas, but we all had to work decorating the room for the tree and program the night all the parents would come. Mama said that our studies must not stop, so each pupil must show each day that he learned some lessons before he could help decorate. By the time for the last recess each day we had all earned the right to work on green and red pasted chains or twisted crepe-paper chains or Christmas posters for the walls or little cut-out figures for the tree. A big girl named Myrtle Farmer made a star and put silver tinfoil on it. A boy named Tots, who could draw real good, made beautiful scenes on the blackboards with colored chalk. Some girls got to string popcorn which Mama popped, and we all teased them and accused them of eating some.

During those days Mama changed our breakfast Bible reading too. Each morning in our room when we washed our hands and sat down to eat, she would read a few verses, then say a short prayer. Usually she read straight through the Bible, including somebody begat somebody and they begat somebody else. Then we would eat our oatmeal with canned milk and maybe have hot chocolate. Now she skipped over to Isaiah and explained that it meant that Jesus was coming. Three days before Christmas she started reading about the Christ in the New Testament.

The last school day before the holiday was the day to get the tree. Two big boys, Auzy Brown and Garland Andrews, went to hunt it on a creek a long way off. They had got their Algebra and other lessons caught up, so they left early. The only trees with leaves were chaparral bushes, but Mama said leaves didn't matter, except we had to have a tree that could come in the door and would not to be too high for the ceiling. The smaller boys could not go, because the big boys were taking an axe. We watched from the schoolhouse hill and when we saw them dragging the tree over the prairie, we ran to help bring it. We struggled and pushed from every side to get it in the door and stood up. Later in the day some boys went to get mistletoe.

Mama had a habit of going with a coal oil lamp into the schoolroom to work on her college after us kids went to bed. Bill said part of the time she prayed in there and asked God to make her know how to be a good father as well as a mother and to be a good teacher of young minds. Bill could have been wrong; a boy of nine is not so smart, but it could be true. Anyway, before the holidays Mama practiced on the organ at night in her spare time. She could play good enough for us to sing in school, but she was afraid Mrs. Meaders, the lady who usually played for community programs, would not get over her flu before Christmas, so she had to be ready. We would lay in bed nearly asleep and listen to her away over there in the other half of the schoolhouse, softly playing, "Oh, Little Town of Bethlehem" and "Silent Night."

On Christmas Eve morning before breakfast Mama said we would read a little more than usual. She read: "And there were in the same country shepherds abiding in the field, keeping watch over their flock by night. And, lo, the angel of the Lord came upon them, and the glory of the Lord shone round about them; and they were sore afraid. And the angel said unto them, Fear not: for, behold, I bring you good tidings of great joy, which shall be to all people." And she read all of it about the shepherds coming to visit the new baby Jesus.

After breakfast we started wrapping presents, each one working in a different place, me on one bed, Mama on one, and Bill behind the kitchen curtain, to keep the presents a surprise. Roy tried to play with his caterpillar tractor, which now had the spring broken and one track lost. Then he played with the stove wood some. Finally he stood out in the middle of the room and started bawling.

After a minute Mama went over to him and asked, "What's the matter, honey? Don't cry."

He didn't want to say. She knelt down and petted him and kept saying, "Don't cry. What's the matter?"

Finally he said, "I love you, Mama."

"I know you do, honey. Don't cry."

"I would give you my tractor, but you already seen it and it wouldn't be a surprise."

She got the whole story out of him and said, "I ought to spank you good." But she smiled a little and went to her purse hanging on the nail. She got out a nickel for him to buy her a present and asked me if I would go down to the store with him.

We put on our coats. Roy no sooner got out the door than he started running. It was about a minute run to the store. Before we got there he was laughing and talking just like he'd never done anything wrong in his life. He bought Mama a Peanut Pattie candy bar about the size of a pancake, only thicker, with peanuts sticking out of the top and wrapped in clear paper.

On the way back up the hill he began to open the sack and I said, "What are you doing?"

"Nothing, I'm just going to look at it."

I said, "Leave it in the sack. What are you doing?" I had thought at first that it was useless for me to go with him, since there are no rattlesnakes in winter and you won't get on a cactus if you stay in the road; but it was a good thing I went—to protect Mama's present.

He said, "I just want to smell of it."

"Roy," I told him, "don't you unwrap that! What do you think you're doing?"

"I'm just going to take a little bite. Mama won't care."

"Don't you dare! Haven't you got a lick of sense?" I got tough with him. "You put that back in that sack and don't you touch it! I'll knock you right on the seat of your pants!"

He knew I meant it. I watched him all the way home and until he got it wrapped in red paper and tied with a string and had put Mama's name on it.

God did not send us a white Christmas that day, but the air was still and cold and clear, like you could see a hundred miles. Later, when dark came, the sky was like purple velvet and the stars were like diamonds, and you could imagine looking up there that you could hear the tune of "Silent Night."

Mama had pumped up and lighted the two gasoline lanterns in the schoolroom, and the schoolhouse hill seemed the most wonderful place a person could possibly be when the people started coming in across the prairie from every direction, driving and walking, most of them laughing. There must have been a hundred, or at least forty. They brought presents to put on the tree for each other. Everyone said how great the schoolroom looked with all our decoration.

It looked as good as a five and ten cent store, not so shiny, but happier. Our chains and ribbons, mostly red and green, looped

103
❧
Benjamin Capps

around on the walls, and the popcorn looked like snow. It was a whole roomful of people, all smiling, and everyone talking at once, until the program started. The lady with the flu was well, so she played the pedal organ and Mama announced. We all sang "Jingle Bells" and other songs. Then the kids who had practiced up gave readings. Two girls and a boy, who could sing good together, sang "Hark, the Herald Angels Sing." Bill, who was good at memory, said, "Twas the Night Before Christmas."

When Santa Claus came in, dressed in red and white, saying, "Ho! Ho! Ho! Have all you boys and girls been good this year?" it was thrilling, but us big kids knew it was Mr. Charlie Graham dressed up that way. The dumb little kids like Roy thought he had just got in on his sled from the North Pole. I had learned about Santa Claus a long time ago, before our daddy died. I even knew where Mama kept the red suit and beard, in a box on top of the green metal bookcase.

The program lasted real late, at least till ten o'clock. All the grown people told Mama thank you before they left. You could hear their voices and laughter going away into the clear, cold night. When we got in our room, after we had looked at our gifts a minute, Roy began talking about hanging up stockings; he'd been talking to the other kids about it.

Mama said, "Boys, we've had a big Christmas. I don't think we need to hang up our stockings this year. We will have some goodies to eat in the next few days."

Roy said, "Well, I want to hang mine up."

"We've had a big Christmas," she said. "Don't you think we should just go to bed and have a good, lazy night's sleep?"

He didn't know what she meant about getting a night's sleep; she meant she didn't have to practice the organ or do any college lessons tonight and she didn't want any other duties in her spare time. See, she had several things to do all the time, being principal, like getting the trustees to haul firewood and getting all the right textbooks and getting chalk and stuff, then keeping up with all the lessons with two in highschool, and making state reports, and getting the broken window fixed, and entertaining the community, and practicing the organ, and furthering her education, and doing all the things mama's like to do such as wash clothes and cook oatmeal and make stew and put patches on your overalls. So she said to us, like it was the last word, "Well, I'm going to bed. Tomorrow I'm going to bake chicken and make dressing." Me and Bill sniggered.

Roy, that dumb kid, took his socks up to the curtain which marked off the kitchen, got two clothes pins, stood on a chair, and hung his socks to the top of the curtain. I could read his dumb mind; this was between him and Santa Claus. After Mama blew out the lamp, me and Bill lay there laughing. Boy, was that kid going to learn something! If your mama says Old Santa Claus ain't coming, then he sure ain't coming anymore tonight! I would have laughed forever if I hadn't been so sleepy.

We nearly always waked up when Mama was building the fire in the morning, because the stove clanked. When she saw us sitting up in bed, she said, "Christmas gift!" It was a joke meaning you had to give them a gift if they said it first, but nobody really did it. Suddenly Roy hopped out of bed and ran toward his socks. I and Bill got to sniggering again.

About that time Roy squealed. His socks were so full he had to take them down one at a time. He ran and started spilling goodies out onto the bed.

Me and Bill looked at Mama. Why in the world had she done that? How could she be such a traitor? It wasn't fair. We liked candy and things as much as him, and he was the one who hadn't acted grown up, but he got a reward for being dumb.

"Jump up, lazy bones," Mama said to me and Bill. How could she be so cheerful when she had acted like a traitor to us? "It's a nice day," she said. "Get your clothes on."

I didn't even want to speak to her as I walked over the cold floor to the chair where I left my clothes. A crazy thought was going through my mind: Could it be possible that there really is a Santa Claus who fills up the stockings of dumb little kids? I got my shoes and socks out from under the chair. I couldn't get my socks on. Something was the matter with them. Lumpy. I nearly cried as old as I was because my mind was still going over the idea if there is really a Santa Claus for dumb little kids.

In my socks was one orange, one apple, fourteen pecans, nine little pieces of hard candy, one big piece of wavy ribbon candy, eleven English walnuts, four Brazil nuts, twelve almonds, and a third of a Peanut Pattie.

We all offered Mama a piece of our candy, and she said she would take a small piece of peppermint, because she didn't care for anything that was too sweet. When she got a chance, she winked at me and Bill. I believe it was a year before Roy ever figured out how come Old Santa Claus put a third of a Peanut Pattie in his sock that night.

105

Benjamin Capps

The Goat of Christmas Past

W E PASSED THE WINTER OF '42 OUT ON THE HIGHWAY IN FRONT of the mountain, in a tiny trailer house that shook in the wind of all that desolation, Uncle John every day falling deeper into the Second Book of Samuel and his second bottle of Jack Daniel while I played solitaire—not with cards but with the primeval play of hawk and cloud and dog and burrow, mesa, butte and arroyo.

Happiness was not, as our streamers and pitiful little signs suggested, a retreat on Mount Morning Air. It was a broad and beautiful mountain, maybe 4,000 feet high and flat enough on top for, say, the sacrifice of a hundred virgin maidens, but it wasn't what anyone in their right mind would call prime property. It was three miles of asphalt on Ranch Rd. 118 near Nine Point Mesa, about midway between Alpine and the ghost town of Terlingua. That stretch of highway is, even today, 70 miles of nothing. Forty years ago it was absolutely nowhere. Magnificent scenery. A good place to hide, but who would want to live there? History said no one and prehistory seemed to suggest the same thing. The mountain had been there for millions of years, unperturbed but for the elements, pretty much left alone by beast and man until Uncle John came along.

"I'm going to develop it," he said.

"What for?" we wanted to know.

"Retired people," he said, "people who want to get away from it all."

Uncle John was a man ahead of his time. And he was excited about his vision. Every year, more and more people were passing through on their way to Big Bend Park, which the state was about to turn over to the federal government for even greater expansion. Brewster County was bound to become a tourist mecca, and that winter, when I had just turned 10, Uncle John threw up two gasoline pumps and dozens of road signs and miles of ribbon inviting travelers to stop and gas up and look at the lots he had staked off on the mountain. There was more than a week to go until Christmas, so Uncle John roared into town in his old Nash to place an ad in the Alpine *Avalanche* inviting everyone to our "gala Christmas opening."

Uncle John came back with balloons, cartons of Coke, a hock shop drum and trombone and a galley proof of the ad he had placed in the paper.

"What's the drum and horn for?" I asked.

"To greet every hundredth customer," he said. "make a big ta-do over it. Get their picture in the paper."

Now I was just a kid, but there were times when I didn't mind correcting Uncle John if I saw him heading hell-bent for disappointment. Gently, I pointed out that there weren't a hundred potential customers, within a hundred miles. Besides, we only had 50 lots. Hadn't we better go ahead and root and toot for every sucker that showed up, just to cover our bets?

Uncle John studied that over and said I was right. We'd give everybody the big treatment.

Well, we went ahead and fudged, opened early, sat out there in front of the trailer house freezing our tails off in the hard, dry air, and I swear to God didn't see but two pickups pass in two days.

A day or so later, as I was stretching my legs hunting arrowheads on the mountain, I saw the tiny speck of a man and what appeared to be a dog following him making their way toward us on the far horizon of the highway. I ran down to Uncle John and pointed them out.

He took his binoculars and focused on the figures. "Now it came to pass," he said, "that after the death of Saul, when David was returned, now it came to pass that, behold, a man came out of the camp with his clothes rent, and earth upon his head. . ."

"Friend or foe?" I asked.

Uncle John put down his spyglasses. "What does it matter?" he shouted. "He's a sight for sore eyes."

March out the band, he ordered. I beat the drum and blew the horn and we went to greet what turned out to be a very startled and exhausted tramp who was in tow with a baby billy goat.

He was as glad to see us as we were to see him, and he fell into our arms, sweating in all that cold and almost swooning. We carried him to the trailer and revived him with a shot of whiskey.

"You've come to buy a lot?" Uncle John began warmly.

"A what?"

"A lot, a retreat on the mountain."

"No," the tramp said, "I don't know what you're talking about."

"Well, why did you come to see us?" Uncle John asked.

The tramp looked at him strangely. "I haven't come to see you," he said. "I am trying to get to Castalon for Christmas. I've been up in the

Davis Mountains. I'm running behind time because I've had to walk every inch of the way. Nobody'll pick me up because of that damned goat. He started following me out of Balmorhea and he's dogged me every step of the way. It's put me in a bad humor, and I've got a bad case of the chills and fever to boot."

Uncle John was looking longingly at the billy. "He's a nice eatin' size," he said, "just right for cabrito."

The tramp nodded appreciatively. "I was going to keep him and eat him when I get to the border," he said, sniffing. "But, friend, I tell you what. You put me up for the night and feed me, toddy me up good for the road, and the goat is yours. He'll make a mighty nice Christmas dinner. I hate to let him go, but without him I can probably catch a trucker."

"My house is your house," Uncle John said.

It took him two days to get up and about, but, sure enough, the tramp hailed a ride on a cattle truck and was gone.

I guess everything would have been fine if I hadn't got to looking at that goat's eyes. I had eaten cabrito all my life, and agreed with the Mexicans that it was a delicacy beyond compare. But most of the goats we had slaughtered had been scraggly-looking critters that looked relieved to be put out of their misery. But this billy was different. He was white with black spots, or black with white spots. Whatever, he was about the cutest thing I had ever seen. The way he wiggled his nose and his tail was a sight. And the tramp was right. He would follow you around all day, looking at you with bright, pink eyes that had the longest white lashes.

I wanted to go play with him up on the mountain, but Uncle John said no, too much exercise would make him tough. "Let's stake him outside and feed him fat for the next few days." he said. "Then we'll barbecue him Christmas Eve and eat him Christmas day."

Uncle John got out his long butcher knife and laid the whetstone to it until it glistened.

I looked at Billy and shivered.

Uncle John shivered too. "I'm comin' down with something awful," he croaked, looking at me with his bleary old eyes. I felt of his forehead.

"Why you're burning up with fever," I said.

"I guess it's the flu," he said. "I musta got it from the tramp. Boy, I feel rotten, all of a sudden. I guess I better put myself to bed so's I'll be up for Christmas."

Uncle John stayed stove up in the back of the trailer, sleeping day and night, awaking only to take aspirin and whiskey. Free of him, Billy and I became fast friends. We played outside all over creation, and at night I slept on the living room couch with the goat beside me. Thus we passed the time. It was wonderful, but I knew with dread what Christmas would bring and after a while it was only a day away. I could see Uncle John taking his long silver sliver and slicing it across Billy's gullet. I could hear the child-like cry, see the red flow gurgling from the white throat.

It was then that I resolved to save Billy from the barbecue pit. I wasted no time. I got up on the eve of Christmas Eve and got some cough syrup that my mother had left me. The bottle was half empty, so I took it to the sink and poured its contents into a bowl. I felt like a witch at her cauldron, and my intent was almost as malevolent as it was benevolent. I was not going to kill Uncle John to spare the goat, but I damned sure was going to knock him out for a spell. I can't remember now, after all these years, exactly what I put into that concoction, but I laced the old cough syrup most powerfully. I know I dissolved a tin of aspirin in it. I know it had whiskey and Coke. I remember some Listerine, some pepper and Tabasco and Worcestershire and sassafras root. But the kicker was a touch of gasoline and turpentine, just dry vermouth enough to take the breath away and roll the eyes back in the head when you touched it to your tongue. Then, for good measure, I crumped up the airy body of a long-dead and very dry tarantula and mixed it in with the rest.

I loved Uncle John, and so I was careful not to overdo it and end up in Huntsville. When I had it just rot-gut right, I went in and roused Uncle John.

"Listen," I told him, "You're not making much headway on whiskey and aspirin. Howabout me giving you some of that cough syrup that Ma left for me. It's real strong."

"Go ahead," he said, "I sure as hell need something."

"Open wide," I said.

"Lord Gawd A'Mighty!" he wheezed, bugging out his eyes as the potion went down. "I've never tasted anything so terrible in all my life. It's like swallowing lava."

"More," I urged him. "Let's try some more, just to be sure."

He slept like a drunk. He slept that night and on into Christmas Eve. Once in a while, I would go in to check on him to make sure he was still breathing. Mostly, I sat outside the trailer house with Billy in my arms, keeping my eyes peeled on the highway and praying. I had put up a sign which read, "Free Goat. Nice Christmas present for some kid."

Most of the time in those days I prayed for the war to be over and for Uncle Glen to come home not all shot up. General Electric's Christmas message was repeated over and over on the radio by movie stars. Bob Hope kept saying it in spot after spot. It went like this: "Christmas is a light no war will dim. It glows in the heart of every man in the armed forces of the United States; it glows in the hearts of those who gather scrap, who use less sugar and coffee and tea and meat, who walk to save gasoline and tires, who keep on buying more war bonds."

But out there on Christmas Eve in Brewster County, I leaned against the trailer house and said a new prayer. "Dear Lord," I said, "Please send somebody out here to take Billy Goat before Uncle John wakes up. Please God, don't let him die, and don't let him kill me either."

It could have been chance, it could have been, perhaps, divine intercession. It didn't matter. A truck appeared on the horizon. It grew larger and louder. It turned into the driveway and stopped before our pumps. And a few minutes later, it pulled away, taking Billy with it.

I lied to Uncle John. I told him the goat had run away in the night. Uncle John wasn't feeling too perky, but he gamely tried to make a holiday of it anyway. We drove into Alpine and had Christmas dinner at a cafe. Turkey and dressing.

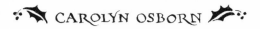

A Christmas Survival Kit

(Containing: decorations, despair, certain memories, music, gifts, relatives, dinner, and a do-right man.)

TACKY GOLD TINSEL SWAGS OVER CONGRESS AVENUE. ALL MY NEIGH-bors find their plastic wreaths yet another year. Several of them are dizzy after running around gas lightpoles wrapping them with broad bands. According to a popular local delusion, red and white tape turns iron poles into candy canes. My landlady Mrs. Gaither, the only person who lives at street level—the rest of the rent apartments tucked in crannies in the cliff below her house—hosed off her aluminum tree this morning. Tied upside down, it's hanging out to dry on her clothesline now while she sorts through boxes of ornaments. I dread the appearance of the stuffed deer head with its red light bulb that blinks on the doorway of the people up the street a block. This very dead Rudolph, magnificently wreathed in green spruce each year, draws admirers from all over Austin and sends me shrieking to my own bare door.

I used to think that no one but merchants liked Christmas; now I must say some of us merchants don't enjoy it either. This is the time my elderly customers panic. They've been sewing sequins on sixteen foot tablecloths, or sticking fake pearls in styrofoam balls, or stringing ropes of glass beads for months. Now, when they've almost finished, each one invariably discovers she's lost twenty or thirty sequins, pearls, or beads.

"The cat likes to play with them."

"Do you suppose a parakeet would swallow—?"

"Must have vacuumed them up."

"Cracks in the floor."

"My grandchild needed something to play with."

"I'm getting so careless."

"So farsighted."

"Forgetful."

"Old."

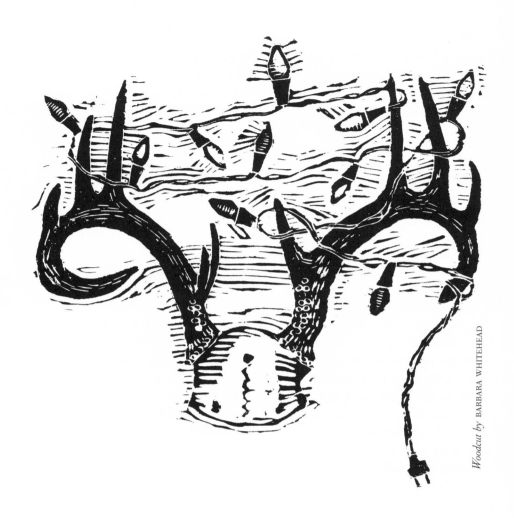

Woodcut by BARBARA WHITEHEAD

I could hide behind the counter and cry for them, but they wouldn't like that. No one willingly accepts pity; however, they are happy for help. They bring their projects. I get out jars of baubles and everyone finishes up amidst mutual admiration of each other's junk. After two days spent working together in the back storage room, they form a Krafts Klub. Never—not for all the sequins in Italy—would they think to name themselves the Crafts Club. Kitsch is kute. I find myself admiring their steadfastness, sitting down with them at tea time—the nexus of any group is food—nibbling Mrs. Murphee's hand-painted cookies, Mrs. Brodie's rum balls, Mrs. Rather's pralines, wondering why they don't put krafts aside and open a candy store instead.

Cooking is their true craft, but these three ladies have no one to cook for any longer except at Christmas when they arrive at their children's homes laden with boxes of sweets and sparkling offerings. The idea makes me sad. Christmas makes me sad.

Here where I have kits for making potholders, stuffed animals, rugs, airplanes, miniature windmills, and wall hangings—every single unnecessary thing in the world—why don't I have a Christmas survival kit? That's what I really need.

On the way to my apartment that evening I remember, as I usually do, it's the winter solstice, a good reason to get dreary. The dark days. The dormant period, a season of less light, less greenery. No wonder our pagan ancestors hauled in the yule log and came home clutching holly. Determined to be more cheerful, I turn on every lamp I own. An hour later a clammy gray cloud oozes through the transom, falls over my head, knots itself into a cold lump, and I wander about wearing despair like a pendant around my neck again.

Do I wish I were a child still? Do I want to believe there really is a Santa Claus? No. I didn't like Christmas even when I was a child.

"Why ever not?" Mrs. Gaither asks when I stop by her place for coffee the next morning. Her tone is one of practical disbelief. Since her childhood is further away than mine, her memories are perhaps as rosy as the pink balls she's hanging on her glittering tree. It's likely that Mrs. Gaither subscribes to the everyone-had-a-happy-childhood myth. Also, because she knows I'm divorced, she's just as likely to attribute every sorrow to that one fact. (The greatest benefit of my divorce—besides parting from a classic ne'er do well—was that I got to keep this apartment in the center of what remains of old Austin, seven blocks from the lake, five from the capitol. I have my own small garden, French doors leading to it, old wavering glass window panes, a combination of high and low ceilings, and Mrs. G. whose over-simplifications are chronic.)

"Why didn't you like Christmas when you were a child?" Mrs. Gaither asks again and offers me a second cup of coffee.

"I don't know exactly why. Certainly I received the gifts I wanted. I got a Shetland pony, a wristwatch, furry red slippers, Lincoln logs, a dollhouse. I was given boxes of crayons in forty-six different colors, charm bracelets, oil paints, the complete works of Louisa May Alcott. When my brother Jack and I quarrelled over his erector set, I was given one of my own." Reciting these lists in the too bright pink light bouncing off Mrs. Gaither's metal tree, I'm oppressed with the memory of so many gifts. Something disastrous happened to most of them. I leave her bathed in her optimistic glow and drive to my shop with my mind on Christmases past.

The pony, the most spectacular present, turned out to have an evil temper. He couldn't abide a single person or any other horse at our ranch near Leon, the small town where I was trying to grow up. The Shetland ruined my Saturday afternoon visits to the ranch for six weeks. He tried to nip anyone who was nearby. Pinky, the foreman, lost part of a shirt. An uncle lost a paper cup full of bourbon and water.

I spent hours leading the pony away from the front porch steps, his favorite place since that's where I got on and off his back. (I was safe on but when I got off, I was bitten like everyone else.) To discipline the pony, we hit him with our fists on his jaw and spoke to him harshly. The Shetland's habit couldn't be broken. Sometime following the sixth week, he chewed on my father's registered quarterhorse and disappeared. I was told that he ran away and I believed the story because I wanted to.

The wristwatch, another grand gift, was rectangular when I'd hoped for a round one, and those slippers made my long feet look like abominable snowman paws. Lincoln logs have certain built-in limitations of design and never enough roofs, the doll-house lacked a doll family—one was never found to fit it. I quickly lost or broke every one of the forty-six crayons. The charm bracelet's jangle made me nervous. After one glorious afternoon spent making up my face to look like an Indian's with an undercoat of ocher and alizarin crimson war stripes, oil paints were forbidden until I was sixteen and no longer particularly interested. Louisa May Alcott's books I rather liked except for their pervasive air of dutifulness which made me wary. And, by the time my parents decided I must have an erector set of my own, I learned that I truly enjoyed quarreling with my brother about the best sort of bridge to build with his.

The gifts were not misguided. There was simply too great a gap between expectations and realities, a crevasse I dug myself. Now that Santa Claus is replaced with immoderate hopes of peace and foolish expectations of joy at least one day of the year, the crevasse deepens. Most of my adult friends also have private sloughs of despond they fall into every December. How are we to keep from wallowing in them?

Maybe Roselle, my friend who runs Wildflowers, the shop across the street from mine, has learned some way out.

"Keep busy," she mumbles. She has a piece of floral wire in her mouth and can barely be seen behind an extravagant arrangement of

Carolyn
Osborn

holly, red velvet birds, and white carnations springing out of a silver wine cooler.

She wires a bird and thrusts him in the cooler. "You know, every year I say I'm going to close this place at Christmas but I never do it. Instead I over-work." She sighs and runs one hand through her long blonde hair. Roselle is one of those people who looks like a princess yet works like a peasant.

"You want to come help direct traffic tonight out at the mall?" Jack asks while playing the melody of a Handel cantata with one hand. He announced earlier this week that he would not play a single carol. "If you want to get good and sick of Christmas, hire out as a security guard at a department store and watch for shop-lifters eight hours a day while being pounded on both ears with 'Come All Ye Faithful.' I can tell you what's on all the muzak tracks in every shopping center in town. The sound of horns and screeching tires is music to my ears."

Ordinarily he's a plain policeman who is also a marvelous pianist. Roselle inherited the old Steinway upright he's playing. She can't play it; however, she keeps the piano tuned for anyone who can. When he's off duty Jack drops in to practice. It's an arrangement that pleases everyone, but I'm not pacified by Handel today. Everybody knows about staying busy. That's not my problem.

"Roselle, you know I keep my shop open till 9 p.m. every night. I've run out of red glitter already. People seem to be dusting it around like sugar. And the macrame workers are tying the world in knots. I can't keep string in the store. Half my time is spent waiting on people and the other half is spent on the telephone talking to suppliers. What I really dread is the day I close the shop and go home to see my family."

Roselle nods sympathetically. She has a large troublesome family in West Texas that doesn't understand why she prefers to remain single at twenty-eight just as my family in Central Texas doesn't understand why I'm not remarried at thirty-nine. Actually geography has nothing to do with it. Both our mothers have an incessant urge to meddle, one that's generally repressed until Christmas, their stock-taking time. And it's unfair to complain just against mothers. Families are such odd mixtures of people with such particular habits, expectations, and eccentricities.

"I don't know about your family, but when mine circles around a table, everyone tends to assert themselves. No matter how hospitable my parents are, someone will leave the house angry."

"There's a cure for bad actors in families," says Jack.

"What?" Roselle and I chorus.

"Always have a stranger in your midst. Everyone is much kinder if there's a stranger around. Two or three or even better."

"Have you ever—?"

"Yes. It's not hard to find people who need a place to go on Christmas, especially if you're a policeman."

"You mean derelicts?" I'm trying to be charitable and finding it hard. Baskets to the poor, my parents would go along with, but bums for Christmas dinner would make them uncomfortable. This realization makes me gloomier than before.

"Margaret, why do you think any self-respecting bum would want to be entertained by a middle-class family?"

"It's my Lady Bountiful complex."

"They'd rather go to the Salvation Army any day. Still there are lots of other lonely people who have no particular plans."

"What are you going to do this Christmas, Jack?"

"I thought you'd never ask."

If Jack went home with me, what would Roselle do? She'd already made her plans. Tom, her current lover, was going home with her. He didn't wear pajamas, wrote vegetarian cookbooks, and was interested in Marxist economics. She trusted his shock value. Everyone would be so busy talking about him for two or three days that the word "marriage" wouldn't even be whispered.

"So, where are we going?" Jack said.

"To Leon."

"After Ponce de?"

"No, after Alfonso de, another Spanish explorer."

He's always curious about place names. That's what brought him to Texas, the name of a town and a uncle who lived there. Eagle Pass sounded to Jack like a place between high windy crags with eagles zooming through them. When he arrived he found a flat, dusty border town. There were no eagles. Were there ever any? Instead of crags he saw pecan groves, spinach farms, ranches. You'd think he'd be disillusioned, but he isn't. Eagle Pass remains exotic to Jack. He likes the sound of Spanish in the streets, the sight of the Rio Grande, shallow and muddy as it is, curving past his uncle's farm.

"I like the contrasts," he insists. Most of his life he's lived in Massachusetts. "I like the heat."

"There are a lot of hot places—Mississippi, Arizona, Southern California." I would have gone on, but he stopped me.

"I don't have an uncle in any of those."

What kind of person chooses to move because of a town's name and one relative? What kind of person decides to make his living being a policeman even though he's a fine pianist?

"You must know that jobs for pianists are limited, Margaret. Look, I got out of college with a degree in fine arts and good training in running cross country races. For awhile I worked as a waiter, then I was a shoe salesman. I came down here to see my uncle who's a retired Texas Ranger. Since I wanted to stay and had to find something to do, he suggested the police force. It all fell in place."

He finds things in place while I'm able to see only a bizzarre chain of circumstance. Perhaps other people's puzzles make sense to them alone. To me Jack is a romantic pragmatist, a paradox which pleases him though it's certain to confound my family. They like for people to be one thing or another.

When we arrive in Leon they can't imagine why I've brought him home unless we intend to marry, so everyone is extra careful at first while Jack goes on acting himself. He drinks the eggnog my father has made—he makes it from scratch before breakfast every Christmas morning and spikes it heavily with brandy. Eggnog, I've come to realize, is my father's method of dealing with his own seasonal miseries. Jack pronounces it the best he's ever had. It is the only he's ever had; however, he's fully aware of the discriminations one ought not to make and doesn't mention his lack of expertise. He helps my brother, also named Jack, add leaves to the dining table and asks intelligent questions about his work at the Marine Science Institute. Our Jack is all too happy to talk about sea-grass and stable bay basins for the next hour. Louise, my sister-in-law, a skinny, wistful looking woman, has a new person to complain to about year-round living on the Texas coast.

"The horizon never changes. There's always this long straight line." Louise can be a number one whiner.

"Must be hypnotic," Jack offers.

"They call it the third coast. Big deal. It's just the Gulf of Mexico sloshing around like water in a big old saucer. Slip-slop. Slip-slop."

Jack looks at her with true interest. "Can you really hear it doing that? In Massachusetts we get mainly crash, rattle, rattle, crash."

In the kitchen Mother, who jumps to conclusions like a parachutist jumps out of a plane asks, "Do you think you'll marry him?"

Well prepared beforehand to be an expert witness in my own defense, I trot out my negations. "No. Jack's only a friend, somebody a

117

Carolyn
Osborn

long way from home on Christmas. It's too expensive for him to fly up to Massachusetts, especially when he doesn't get much time off."

"He seems to be a nice young man."

"Young is right. He's twelve years younger than I am, and I have no designs on him. He's a musician, a pianist."

"He told your father he was a policeman." Mother looks at me to see if I know my friend Jack is a liar. At the same time she rattles a tray full of silverware indicating she wants me to set the table.

"He knows father is a district judge so he told him what would interest him most. He's both a policeman and a musician. And, for heaven's sake, Mother, don't ask him to play *Silent Night*."

"Why not? It's Christmas, isn't it?"

"He's had to listen to carols all day long in shopping centers and is sick of them. How is Cicily?"

"All right. She called last night. Said to thank you for the pajamas. I didn't know she wore them. England's so cold though. I guess she and Bob have taken to red flannels."

They were pet-pajamas for their dog, a dachshund who already owns two coats to wear outside. I do not tell Mother this as I see my sister is being tactful. Mother doesn't approve of the kind of gifts we give. Jack and Louise, Cicily and Bob, and I agreed years ago that we would never agonize over Christmas presents for each other. Now we compete to see who can find the most ludicrous objects. Living in London with Bob who's a member of an import-export firm gives Cicily some advantage as she's got practically the whole world of trash to choose from, but aesthetics always rules her choice. This year she sent me an antique perfume bottle with a blue glass snake coiled around it. As you can see by the pet-pajamas, I specialize in utilitarian tacky. For Jack and Louise I bought something called a "Baker's Dozen Sponge Loaf" which looks like a loaf of sliced bread, but when you open the package you discover a dozen bread-slice-shaped sponges in appalling pinks and greens with brown crust edges. I think that this year's winner was all Louise and Jack could find for me, a wind-up alarm with "Wake Up Margaret!" printed on its face. Their children are a bit on the edge of all this for they are natural trash lovers. However, Karl and Cathy are included on my list. Both of them received monster coloring books featuring Godzilla, King Kong, and Frankenstein which are scattered over the living room floor right now.

"Who else is going to be here for dinner?" I see Mother has furnished silver for two extra places.

"Aunt Ida and— What's he doing?"

From the dining room you can see out the living room windows. Jack is standing on the front walk teaching Karl, 9, motions for traffic signals while Cathy, 7, riding a new red bicycle with training wheels attached, is acting as traffic.

"Oh-h-h," Mother groans. "Get him to quit it before Aunt Ida arrives."

Aunt Ida is Mother's aunt, my great-aunt. She is seventy-three, still driving her car and living in her house alone. All of her working life she was director of activities on passenger ships sailing to and from Europe more times than she can remember and around the world at least twice.

"Why? Aunt Ida loves to see people busy."

"She's taken a dislike to policemen." Mother opens the oven door to feel the smoked venison she's heating. "Ida had an accident last week. She thought her car was in reverse when it was in drive. The car was parked on an incline. So, instead of backing out of her place, she went forward through the window of Millers', the radio-TV-appliance store. She ran over eleven radios, three color TVs, and put a bad dent in a large yellow refrigerator."

"Wonderful!"

"It was not wonderful at all. The sheriff took her to the jail to ask her some questions and had to call your father who had to call me to go get her. She was nearly hysterical. All the way home she cursed. I never heard so many strange curses. 'Hell's blue bells!' Why blue? Anyway she was terribly angry at the sheriff. She thought he was threatening to take her driver's license away." All the time she's talking Mother is doing other things, motioning to me to tear up salad greens, unmolding a gelatin ring, sticking dishes in the washer, making coffee, lifting a lid to sniff green beans. It's a tremendous juggling act accompanied by patter.

"Well, at least Aunt Ida learned something beside how to organize dances and play shuffle-board all those years she was at sea." I go on tearing up crisp lettuce leaves. "You still haven't said who the other place is for."

"Cousin Robert." She pretends the rice needs poking and lifts the lid so a cloud of steam rises over her face.

"For Christmas! Why can't he go to his own parents' house?" I cover the lettuce with a towel and push the bowl in the refrigerator as though it was Cousin Robert I'm putting on ice. Of all the people in our family, he's the one I dislike the most, but there's no use discussing my feeling about him. Robert is her sister's son, so Mother won't admit he's a terrible person. The most she's ever said is, "He's troubled." If he was caught shooting someone on the square at mid-day or discovered hauling a tow sack full of heroin down Main, Mother would only wail, "He's always had problems." Kinship is a protective cloud cover she throws over her entire family.

At dinner I sit next to my father who looks rather magisterial at the head of the table. Benevolent and brandy warmed, he presides. Then there's Aunt Ida, Cousin Robert, who ought not to be here at all, Louise, Karl, Jack parting his two children, Cathy, Mother, and Jack, the stranger in our midst.

"Well, young man, what do you do?" After years of entertaining strangers, Aunt Ida wastes no time on preliminaries.

"He plays the piano." I intrude before Jack can answer.

"After lunch maybe you can jingle some bells for us." She means to sound like a jolly good sport. On the whole she is, but her heartiness is false. Immediately after dinner Aunt Ida will take a nap as usual, and as usual we'll all have to help her look for something before she goes home—she'll lose her brooch, or her glasses, or her housekey. It has happened every Christmas since her retirement; Aunt Ida's losses and the hunts which follow are as traditional as the star on top of the tree. Following the nap and the hunt, she'll have one glass of sherry and someone will have to drive her home.

"You won't want any bells ringing while you're napping, Aunt Ida."

That's Robert. Mean. He's thirty-six, hawk-faced, razor-tongued, unmarried, and liable to stay that way. He manages Wesson's, his father's department store. Otherwise, he'd probably be wanted for mail fraud or some other dreary con game. I often think I see Robert's face on Post Office wanted posters.

"Where are your parents, Robert?" I ask only because he needs to be led away from Aunt Ida.

"They went on a cruise to the West Indies and left me to mind the store. For the last two weeks all I've seen of them is a lot of sunshiny postcards."

"Well, when they get back you can take off awhile." Mother, as usual, tries to placate.

Aunt Ida raises her head and issues an authoritarian pronouncement, "They will return well-rested."

"You ought to know, Ida, restful cruises are travel agent myths. Mother and Father dance all night, tour an island a day, and when they aren't dancing or touring they're shopping. Mother is a compulsive shopper. In between these activities they swim in an ocean of rum. They're going to come home looking like two tubs."

My father raises his eyes from his plate as if to say, "I told your mother not to ask Robert." Then he coughs slightly and changes the subject, his favorite diversionary tactic. "Clara, you did a beautiful job cooking this venison."

Cathy asks, "What's venison?" She's a model of a delightful looking granddaughter—pixie face, large brown eyes, dark curly hair bouncing in a pony tail.

Karl answers, "Deer meat, silly."

"Rudolph!" Cathy wails and drops her fork on the carpet. "I'm eating Rudolph!"

My father, by a glance, tells me he is disconcerted by her ignorance but will not call attention to it.

I lean toward him and whisper, "After dinner let's drive out to the ranch and shoot Peter Cottontail, and Bambi, and all the rest of the gang."

"Hush, honey." Louise commands her daughter in her most soothing voice, "You don't have to eat him."

"Look here, Cathy." Robert grabs his ice water and gulps half of it down. "I'm drinking Frosty the Snowman and it doesn't hurt him a bit. Plenty more, isn't there, Aunt Clara?"

Mother takes this as a hint to refill Robert's glass. Before I can stop her she's in the kitchen knocking ice cubes out of a tray. She thinks she can quell his meanness by catering to him. I would kick Robert under the table as I did when were both children, but it's a big table, and he's too far away, and a kick wouldn't cure him.

For a few minutes everyone quits eating to listen to my brother. "It's not Rudolph, honey. This is deer meat. Rudolph's a reindeer. He lives way up by the North Pole. This kind of deer lives in Texas. You've seen them out at the ranch. They don't have anything to do with Santa Claus." He sighs. It's hard for a scientist to justify belief in fictional animals. We can tell by his tone, however, that he's accustomed to explaining things to his daughter. We can also tell that his explanation isn't satisfactory; Cathy's tears still drip on her plate.

My father begins to look slightly guilty, Robert grins, Aunt Ida is perplexed. She's spent so much of her life arranging adult games she's forgotten childish fantasies. Louise holds her head between both hands. Mother runs around the table filling water glasses. Jack eats his venison and winks at me. I wish he'd find something more useful to

Carolyn
Osborn

do, but there he sits, my buffer zone, the stranger who was going to put everyone on their best behavior.

"Here," Karl says, pushing his plate toward his sister, "Put it on mine." He's already accepted his elder child job. Both of his parents smile on him. Cathy does as he suggests and, mercifully, quits crying.

When mother passes the fruitcake and decorated cookies later, Cathy takes a Santa Claus cookie, admires him for a few minutes, then bites off his head without a murmur.

My father leans over his port glass and says to me, "My granddaughter, the cannibal."

"If you'll write that up, I think it'll sell." This comforts him a bit. The deer was a twelve point buck, and he was proud he'd shot him at the ranch. For years we saw plenty of coyotes and jackrabbits out there but no deer. Now hordes have drifted up from South Texas. There are more deer at the ranch than there are people, cows, and horses altogether.

Evidently thinking it's safe to begin a general conversation again, my father turns toward Jack, "What do you find the most dangerous aspect of police work?"

Interfering in family brawls without getting shot or stabbed is Jack's usual reply. Before he can think of some tactful way to say this, Robert breaks in with, "Bad drivers, I bet."

"Police work!" Aunt Ida puffs. "I thought you said he was a pianist, Margaret."

"Right after dinner he's going to take you off to jail." Robert laughs.

"It's the do-right man, the do-right man!" Karl and Cathy chant together like two perfect little toads. They aren't themselves again until Louise quiets them.

Without a word to anyone Jack rises, walks into the living room, sits down at Mother's piano, and begins playing a medley of carols.

"Today he's just a musician, Aunt Ida."

"Tomorrow?" Robert insists.

"We'll be gone." I smile at him as kindly as possible while Jack, the talented stranger, drifts into a Beethoven sonata.

NOTES ABOUT THE AUTHORS

GORDON BAXTER produced and sold his own radio show in the Beaumont-Port Arthur area for thirty-one years. He has been a pilot for a quarter of a century, and has written many books and articles on flying. His book, *Village Creek* ("the first and only eyewitness account of Gordon Baxter") has been especially acclaimed.

ELROY BODE, a native of Kerrville (born 1931), graduated summa cum laude from the University of Texas at Austin. He has taught in public schools, has produced half a dozen books, and has been published in *New Mexico Quarterly*, *Texas Quarterly*, *Texas Observer*, *Redbook*, and elsewhere.

BENJAMIN CAPPS, a resident of Grand Prairie, is widely known as a writer of novels and histories about the American West. He has won the Spur Award (given by the Western Writers of America) three times and has won the Wrangler Award once. His many books include *Woman Chief*, published in 1979.

JOE B. FRANTZ, former chairman of the History Department at the University of Texas at Austin, was consultant in history to the White House during President Johnson's occupancy. He has also been director of the Texas State Historical Association and president of the Western History Association, Southern Historical Association, and Texas Institute of Letters. His *Gail Borden* won the 1951 TIL nonfiction award.

WILLIAM GOYEN, novelist, short-story writer, and playwright, was a reviewer for the *New York Times*, 1950–1975, and has taught at Brown, Columbia, New School for Social Research, and Princeton. An early work, *The House of Breath*, won the 1950 Texas Institute of Letters award for fiction. A version of his story included in this book appeared in *Redbook* in 1979. The story here is © 1983 by William Goyen.

A. C. GREENE, author of *A Personal Country*, has written nonfiction (especially reminiscences and histories) and fiction. He is a former amusements editor of the *Abilene Reporter-News*, book editor and editorial columnist of the *Dallas Times Herald*, and television producer at KERA, Dallas. In recent years his "History According to A. C. Greene" has been heard daily on WFAA Radio, Dallas.

LEON HALE served as humor editor for the first newspaper published at Eastland High School, later graduated with a B.A. from Texas Tech. Currently (and for years now) he has acquired a large following as columnist for the *Houston Post*. His novels include *Bonney's Place* and *Addison*, which won the Texas Institute of Letters fiction award in 1979.

SHELBY HEARON has written nine books, seven of which are novels, including *Afternoon of a Faun* (1983). Born in Kentucky, she lived for many years in Texas, and is a graduate of The University of Texas, has twice won the Texas Institute of Letters award for the year's best novel. She now lives in Westchester County, New York, with her husband, Bill Lucas. Her recent awards include fellowships from the Guggenheim Foundation and the National Endowment for the Arts.

ROLANDO R. HINOJOSA-SMITH, professor of English at the University of Texas at Austin, has written five novels depicting life in the Lower Rio Grande Valley, of which he is a native. In 1976 he won Latin America's prestigious literary award, the Casa de las Americas Prize, and in 1972 he received the National Award for Chicano Literature. His books include *Rites and Witnesses* (1982).

ELMER KELTON has written twenty-four novels over the past twenty-five years. He is twice winner of the Western Heritage Award from the National Cowboy Hall of Fame, for his novels *The Time It Never Rained* and *The Good Old Boys*. He has won the Spur Award from Western Writers of America four times, for *Buffalo Wagons*, *The Day the Cowboys Quit*, *The Time It Never Rained*, and *Eyes of the Hawk*. He lives in San Angelo.

TOM LEA, a native of El Paso (born 1907), studied two years (1924–1926) at the Art Institute, Chicago, and studied anthropology two years (1933–1935) before winning renown as an artist. His career as a muralist, easel painter, and book illustrator dates from 1936. Since 1947 he has written and illustrated eight books, including *The Brave Bulls* (1949) and *In the Crucibles of the Sun* (1974). During World War II he was a combat artist for *Life Magazine*.

STANLEY MARCUS, a native of Dallas (born 1905), received the B.A. degree from Harvard (1925) and studied further in the business school there. His association with Neiman-Marcus began in 1926; he is now chairman of the board, emeritus. He is the author of three books, many magazine articles, and is a member of the Texas Institute of Letters, comprised of authors who have a Texas association.

VASSAR MILLER has lived all her life in Houston, where she was born in 1924. She earned B.S. and M.A. degrees from the University of Houston; was writer-in-residence at the University of Saint Thomas, 1975–

1976. Her poetry was nominated for the Pulitzer Prize in 1961; three books have won annual poetry awards given by the Texas Institute of Letters. Her work has appeared in more than fifty anthologies.

CAROLYN OSBORN, from Nashville, Tennessee, has lived in Texas since 1946. She graduated from the University of Texas at Austin with B.A. and M.A. degrees. Later she taught English there; and has been writer-in-residence at the Universidad de las Americas. She is the author of *A Horse of Another Color* (1977). Her short stories have appeared in *Texas Quarterly*, *New Orleans Review*, *Paris Review*, *Antioch Review*, and elsewhere.

WILLIAM A. OWENS grew up not long after the turn of the century in a Northeast Texas community called Pin Hook, in great poverty. Education acquired as a result of youthful yearning enabled him to reach great heights: schoolteacher, university professor (including many years at Columbia University) and prize-winning author of novels and nonfiction. Among his books are *Look to the River* (fiction) and *This Stubborn Soil* ("an autobiographical chronicle").

BILL PORTERFIELD, formerly on the staff of the *Houston Chronicle* and now a columnist for the *Dallas Times Herald*, was the first recipient of the J. Frank Dobie-Paisano Fellowship for writers. His short pieces have won two awards given by the Texas Institute of Letters, but he is also the author of three books, including *Texas Rhapsody: Memories of a Native Son* (1981).

GENE SHUFORD, known to many persons around his home town of Denton as "Pop," is the author of two books: *Selected Poems* and *1300 Main Street and Other Poems*. He served as 1983 councilor of the Poetry Society of Texas, and in 1982 won second place in the John A. Lubee Awards. Shuford, who has been professor of English at North Texas State University for many years, served one year as alternate Poet Laureate of Texas (1975–1976).

CARROLL HARRIS SIMMS, born in 1924 in Bald Knob, Arkansas, lived with his sister in the home of his maternal grandparents in the days before racial integration was even a dream in that region. He moved to Toledo, Ohio, in 1938 to live with a distant relative and began a pursuit of education that brought him to his current position of professor of art at Texas Southern University. He is a co-author of *Black Art in Houston: The Texas Southern University Experience* (1978).

JACQUELINE SIMON, who received B.S. and M.A. degrees from Louisiana State University, is now a resident of Houston, where she has taught writing at Houston Community College. In 1979 she began writing full time, and in 1981 a story, "Sisters," won a Texas Writer Recognition Award. Another story that same year won first place in fiction in the Houston Discovery Prize Competition sponsored by PEN Southwest.

MARSHALL TERRY, born in Cleveland, Ohio, in 1931, received B.A. and M.A. degrees from Southern Methodist University, where he later became professor of English and chairman of the department. His novel, *Tom Northway*, was a co-winner of the Texas Institute of Letters fiction award in 1968, and his short story, "The Antichrist," won a 1972 TIL award. He resides in Dallas and teaches at SMU.

R. G. VLIET, poet and novelist, was in residence at J. Frank Dobie's old ranch as the current Dobie-Paisano Fellow when he submitted "A Garland." His novel, *Solitudes*, won the 1977 Texas Institute of Letters award for fiction, and his poetry has won TIL prizes, too. In 1969 he was a Rockefeller Fellow in fiction and poetry.

127

Notes

JOHN EDWARD WEEMS, who attended public schools in California, earned B.J. and M.J. degrees (1948 and 1949) from the University of Texas at Austin. His *Dream of Empire* (written with wife Jane as researcher) won the 1971 Texas Institute of Letters award for southwestern history. Two other books on arctic exploration, including the biography *Peary*, were used as the basis of a CBS Television special on the explorer Robert Peary in 1973.

BRYAN WOOLLEY grew up near historic Fort Davis. He earned degrees at the University of Texas at El Paso, Texas Christian University, and Harvard. Currently he is on the staff of the *Dallas Times Herald*. He has a number of books, both fiction and nonfiction, to his credit, including the acclaimed novel, *Some Sweet Day*.

Design:
Whitehead & Whitehead
Typesetting: G & S
Printing:
Thomson-Shore

Drawing by TOM LEA